W9-ADH-416

Praise for *Seven Steps to Inner Power*

"An exciting new voice in self-transformation. Having broken through often-impenetrable barriers to women, the author shows us exactly how to let go of limited ways of thinking and break through every obstacle to our own life goals. *Seven Steps to Inner Power* is a remarkably timely and authentic guide to reaching new heights of happiness and achievement."

—MARCI SHIMOFF, *New York Times* bestselling author of *Happy for No Reason*

"Tae Yun Kim has written an incomparable masterpiece revealing the secrets for the harmonious balancing of body, mind, and spirit in *Seven Steps to Inner Power: How to Break Through to Awesome*. Kim has beautifully authored an impeccable step-by-step manual for personal empowerment, with explicit instructions for those willing to do the work. This book is a new imperative for everyone who desires to become the great grandmaster of their own destiny."

—DANNION BRINKLEY and KATHRYN BRINKLEY, bestselling authors of *Secrets of the Light: Lessons from Heaven*

"An extraordinary woman with an extraordinary story whose profound teachings will convince you that you can be extraordinary too. It's not often I stay up late at night reading a self-help book, but this one was hard to put down. Every page is inspiring and motivating."

—PEGGY McCOLL, *New York Times* bestselling author of *Your Destiny Switch*

"Tae Yun Kim, a female martial arts great grandmaster, presents a unique and candid approach to finding your own truth, standing up for yourself, and making the most of the moments in your life. Drawing on lessons she learned in her training and that she now passes on to her students, she shows why it is essential, at any age, to reevaluate and up the ante on what you believe you are capable of achieving. Her seven steps provide a wise blueprint for seeing goals through to completion and acting with intention to make your entire life a moving meditation. In short, *Seven Steps to Inner Power* is packed with profound truths as well as practical keys for creating deep and meaningful breakthroughs."

—*Common Ground Magazine*

"Whatever stage of life you're in, *Seven Steps to Inner Power: How to Break Through to Awesome* will keep you thinking big and reaching high. Dr. Tae Yun Kim's determination and drive are absolutely contagious. After reading this book, you'll think twice before ever letting another challenge stand in your way again. A beautiful, self-affirming work that you'll want to keep by your side and read again and again."

—*Patricia Spadaro*, author of *Honor Yourself: The Inner Art of Giving and Receiving*

"In *Seven Steps to Inner Power*, great grandmaster Tae Yun Kim shows us that the same power she cultivated to achieve her goals is a power available to everyone—the power of inner strength. No matter where you are on your journey, these seven steps to inner power will give you the focus to bring your inner strength forward."

—*Spirit of Change Magazine*

Seven Steps *to* Inner Power

How to Break Through to Awesome

Seven Steps *to* Inner Power

How to Break Through to Awesome

Life Secrets from a Martial Arts Master

Tae Yun Kim, *Great Grandmaster*

MOUNTAIN TIGER PRESS

Copyright © 2018 Tae Yun Kim. All rights reserved. Printed in the United States of America. No part of this book may be used, reproduced, translated, electronically stored, or transmitted in any manner whatsoever without prior written permission from the publisher, except by reviewers, who may quote brief passages in their reviews.

For information, address:

Mountain Tiger Press
2728 West Main St., #115
Medford, OR 97501
E-mail: info@mountaintigerpress.com

For foreign and translation rights, contact Nigel J. Yorwerth
E-mail: nigel@PublishingCoaches.com

Library of Congress Control Number: 2017919617

ISBN: 978-0-9994282-0-7 (trade paperback)
ISBN: 978-0-9994282-1-4 (e-book)

10 9 8 7 6 5 4 3 2

Cover design: Nita Ybarra
Creative direction and production: Yorwerth Associates, LLC

Some of the names and details in the stories in this book have been changed to protect the privacy of those involved. The information and insights in this book are solely the opinion of the author and should not be considered as a form of therapy, advice, direction, diagnosis, and/or treatment of any kind. This information is not a substitute for medical, psychological, or other professional advice, counseling, or care. All matters pertaining to your individual health should be supervised by a physician or appropriate health-care practitioner. Neither the author nor the publisher assumes any responsibility or liability whatsoever on behalf of any purchaser or reader.

GARY PUBLIC LIBRARY

Blade of grass fluttering in the wind
Breaking rock,
Within.

3 9222 03233 9314

CITY PUBLIC LIBRARY

Contents

PART ONE

The Way
of the Warrior

Chapter One

Breaking Through Barriers

CONSIDER YOUR HAND for a moment. Feel the softness of your skin. Imagine the bones and ligaments within. As you flex your fingers, think of the dexterity of this part of yourself that you so often take for granted.

Can you imagine your hand moving through a brick and breaking it into pieces? Can you imagine your hand breaking through a stack of concrete blocks? Maybe you think that is impossible for you or anyone to accomplish.

I assure you, it *can* be done.

Perhaps you've heard of other amazing and seemingly superhuman feats—the mother who lifted a car with her bare hands to free her son trapped underneath or the two teenage girls who hoisted a three-thousand-pound tractor off of their father, saving his life. Or maybe you've observed in wonder a delicate blade of grass that has broken right through a thick block of cement. How are these feats of power possible? They are possible when we tap into and summon our innate life force, our inner power, with one-pointed, laser-beam focus—when we bring our body, mind, and spirit together as one.

Can you tap into that kind of power in your everyday life? Absolutely. I wrote this book to show you how.

As a grandmaster in the martial arts, what I teach enables people not only to break bricks but to break through the even harder barriers that can block our happiness and fulfillment. You may at first think this means I will teach you to be aggressive or to be a bully. Not at all. When you see that blade of grass sprouting up through cement or a tree growing through solid rock, look carefully. It is the cement or the rock that cracks. Rather than describing the blade of grass and the tree as "aggressive," it is more accurate to say that they are being true to their own lives and purpose. They are being true warriors.

Tapping into your inner power to stay true to your real self is at the root of the martial art I teach, Jung SuWon. That phrase may sound foreign to your ears, but it simply means "the way of uniting body, mind, and spirit in total harmony." How often are our minds somewhere else, thinking, "I've got to do this or that" instead of focusing on the task at hand? How often do we dwell on a past event or worry about the future instead of celebrating the beauty of the moment unfolding right before our eyes? When our minds are distracted by busyness or worry, our energy becomes fragmented in many different directions. These distractions steal our energy. When that happens over and over again, we become weak, ineffective, and even paralyzed. Not only that, but we cannot be true to ourselves.

Freeing Yourself from Limiting States of Mind

While the art of Jung SuWon includes a physical form, it is more than a martial art. It goes far beyond the hard martial art forms that are strictly of foot and fist, and it is not a sport. Jung SuWon embraces principles and practices that help you develop your whole being—body, mind, and spirit. Its mental and spiritual aspects are not separate from its physical form.

Let me give you a quick example. In the martial arts, powerful kicks and punches are worthless unless they are properly directed at an appropriate target with the necessary mental focus. In other words, physical strength is only as good as mental strength. All the physical strength in the world will not help if your mind is full of fear. As students practice, they identify what weaknesses are holding them back. They learn to fight to free themselves from those limitations so they can express their innate power. As they cultivate determination, confidence, and strength in practicing martial arts, they also apply those same qualities to the challenges in their daily lives. They are learning to free themselves from whatever is holding their dreams and their future hostage.

The same principles hold true for you in your everyday life. You must learn to conquer fear and weakness within before you can overcome any foe or obstacle outside of yourself. You must fight for your freedom. Thus, the purpose of the art of Jung SuWon is to give you practical tools to free yourself from limiting, self-defeating states of mind.

This takes practice, but you can do it. You will see the word *practice* many times in this book. After all, Olympic athletes don't win a gold medal in one day. It requires practice. A writer doesn't become great in one day. Great writers practice their skill every day. They know they will become better writers the more they practice. You don't become a good leader overnight. You have to practice your leadership skills, learning to make the right kind of decisions and inspire those you work with to accomplish their goals.

One of the most important ways we practice is with our minds. Going back to the example of the martial arts master who uses his or her hand to break through a stack of cement blocks, do you remember the first time you watched a demonstration like that? You may have gasped in disbelief, thinking that the human hand is so much softer and less dense than a block of cement. Of course it is. But thought is what propels the hand of the martial artist. Thought is also what propels your hand as you go through your daily activities. In fact, isn't it your thought that moves you in any direction and to any purpose throughout your life?

You are already practicing with your mind and thoughts every day, and you are already focusing your energies. The only difference between you and a martial arts master is where and how you focus. Say you have stopped somewhere to admire a sunset, enthralled by nature's breathtaking display of beauty. In that moment, you are focusing with your mind. Say you are training for a sports event or learning to play a musical instrument, practicing yoga, or studying with intense concentration. Again, you're using your mind to focus—to direct your activities and succeed at your chosen task. In this book, I'll share principles and techniques of mental conduct that will enable you to use your inner power to transform your life and break through the real obstacles that are holding you back. For, as you'll hear throughout these pages, *the first step in taking charge of your life is to learn to take charge of your thinking.*

Here's another way of looking at how powerful and transforming it can be when your whole being is focused and in harmony. Do you remember your first kiss? Was it both soft and powerful? Did the sensation lift you off your feet? Did your heart feel like it was going to fly out of your chest? We all remember the moment of our first kiss, no matter how long ago it was. We remember where we were and whose lips caressed our own. Why? We were completely lost in the moment of that new and exciting experience. Our body, mind, and spirit were completely engaged as one. That kiss was the only thing happening in the universe at that moment and we were giving it our full attention.

Practicing the art of Jung SuWon, the art of uniting body,

mind, and spirit in total harmony, is like that too. I want to help you capture that feeling of excitement again. I want to help you fall in love with your life. I want to teach you how to celebrate every breath and direct the power of your whole being toward what you want to accomplish, experience, and express in your life.

You Are More Than Your Environment

To help you better understand the origins of what I teach and why I teach, I would like to relate a few of the key events that influenced my life and led me, through hard-earned experience, to the wisdom I now want to share with you. Although some of the events of my life may have been more intense, difficult, or simply different than what you've experienced, my story is also your story. All of us face challenges, pressures, or obstacles that try to prevent us from becoming our most powerful, most authentic selves. While people and events can shape you, for better or for worse, you do have power over those influences, more power than you realize. It doesn't matter how bad your current circumstances may seem. What I have discovered throughout my life is that *how* I dealt with circumstances was much more important than the circumstances themselves or the environment in which I was raised.

At first, we are all largely products of our surroundings and our environment. Children who grow up in a family where everyone plays music are more likely to become musicians themselves. If you live in the countryside and everyone around you loves to fish, you will probably become an expert fisherman too. A baby born in China to Chinese parents who moves to the United States shortly after birth will look Chinese but grow up speaking and acting as an American because of the environment the child grows up in.

Our environmental influences can be positive or negative, of course, and are often both. If you live in a family of alcoholics or are surrounded by people who are afraid of trying anything new, you may very well take on those habits or traits yourself. However, that does not mean that you are destined to live your entire life like that. That does not mean you are stuck. I am greatly saddened when I meet people who believe it's not possible to go beyond the influences of their environment, who have grown up thinking "This is it—this is all I'll ever amount to for the rest of my life."

I am here to tell you that what you have experienced so far in your life is *not* "it." It's not the end of the story. With the right tools in hand, you can break away from that limited thinking and find a new identity—your own identity. That is why I want to tell you a little of my own story. In order to create the life I desired and uncover my own identity and life purpose, I had to overcome the opinions and judgments of my family as well as a culture that sought to deny me what I wanted out of life.

First you must picture what it was like in the country of my birth in 1946. I was born in a small village of about three hundred people in South Korea. We were surrounded by mountains and rivers. There was no electricity and there were no phones. South Korea was a small country at that time, a society steeped in structured tradition stretching back five thousand years.

One of our many customs was that it was important for the firstborn child in a family to be a boy. That is how families would measure their success, and it was disastrous if the firstborn was a girl. When a boy was born, families would hang a rope laden with hot chili peppers outside the front door. If the newborn was a girl, they hung charcoal outside the door instead. You can see that boys were welcomed into the world much differently than girls were. Just being born female was a disadvantage. Some people even went so far as to drown firstborn baby girls to avoid the stigma of having a firstborn girl.

Not only was I the firstborn child and grandchild in my family, but I was born at the lunar new year, a time when everyone pays respect to their ancestors and asks them to bless the land and give them many grandsons and much abundance. My grandfather was the leader of our village and my grandmother was the perfect Korean woman, having given birth to eight sons and two daughters. Each new year, the people of the village, many of whom were our relatives, would gather in my grandfather's yard to pay respect to their ancestors. So the expectations that his first grandchild would be a boy were great, to say the least. My grandfather was absolutely convinced that on this auspicious day the Kim family would surely be blessed with a healthy baby boy to carry on the family name. There was not so much as a grain of doubt in his mind.

"My grandson is going to have the biggest hot pepper," he bragged to the villagers as he waited for hours outside the house to hear news of my birth. "He's going to rule this country."

When my grandfather heard my first cries, he shouted in to my grandmother: "Woman! Tell me, what is my grandson's hot pepper size?"

My grandmother looked at the tiny little bundle in front of her, realized in dismay that I was not a baby boy sporting a hot pepper, and said to herself, "Oh my God, our family has been cursed. *We're doomed.*" That was my grandmother's first greeting to me, and I would hear those words many times as I grew up.

She was afraid to tell my grandfather the news. When she finally did, he was horrified. In distress, he ran to the family altar in the house and prayed, asking why his family had been cursed with a firstborn girl. All he could say was "What have I done to deserve such bad luck?" Don't we all tend to react like this? We become so attached to what we think is the best outcome that when things don't turn out as we think they should and our high expectations come tumbling to the ground, we get angry and lose our moorings.

The whole village was in shock. To celebrate a birth, the women traditionally cooked a large pot of nourishing seaweed soup to feed the woman who had just given birth and to share with the entire village. In my mother's case, the villagers were so upset to hear I was a girl that they dumped out the soup. "You cannot eat this seaweed soup," they said to my mother. "Your bad luck will be contagious!"

After hearing those superstitious and demeaning comments and seeing what a tiny little thing I was, my mother was so distraught that she didn't want to have anything to do with me. She pushed me in the corner and left me alone, fully expecting me to die. Many hours later, when she saw me moving and making noise, she decided she had to feed me.

So from the moment of my birth, my family and the people of the small South Korean village where I was born called me a curse. From then on, each time my family experienced some hardship, they blamed me as the cause of their bad luck. I grew up being branded a disgrace. My mother, ostracized for not producing a son for the family, in turn blamed me for her difficulties, as did my father. He openly resented the fact that I hadn't turned out to be a boy, and in his alcoholic rages he would beat me and my mother.

Not only that, but no one in the village would talk to me. The children were instructed not to play with me for fear that my bad luck would infect them too. As a child, I was accustomed to people shouting at me all the time. My grandparents, my mother, everyone would say to me: "Don't go there! Don't do that!" I thought that being constantly shouted at was normal.

The Starting Point of Determination

Things only got worse for me and for everyone with the start of the Korean War. Among my earliest memories are those of the chaos and hardship the war brought—the bombing, the shouting, the running. I couldn't understand why the world had suddenly gone crazy, why explosions were happening everywhere, why people would try to hurt me.

Since daughters were considered less valuable than sons and just one more mouth to feed, many families abandoned their daughters during the war and fled with their sons by their sides. One day, in their terror, my family did just that. They ran off, completely abandoning me. I was only five years old. Terrified, I cried out, "Mom, Mom! Where are you? Where are you?" At one point, an old man grabbed my hand and yelled, "Shut up!" (I had a very loud voice even then!) "Come with me," he insisted. "You can't stay here." It was complete chaos. My ears were filled with the noise of the planes flying overhead and the bombs exploding all around me.

I ran to keep up with everyone else, but my short little legs soon couldn't run anymore and I slowed down. Suddenly a girl, who was a few years older than I was, hurried over. I had never seen this girl before, and to this day I have no idea who she was. "You can't stay here," she said urgently. "We have to get out of here. Come on, I'll race you!" I couldn't believe it. In the midst of this inferno, someone, for the first time ever, was nice to me. Her words sounded sweet to my ears. I was so used to people shouting at me that she seemed like an angel. All I wanted to do was please her, so I started running again.

In that moment, I forgot about my mother and everybody else. All I could think about was my new friend. I raced after her with every ounce of energy I could muster and ran hard to keep up with her. I was so tired, but she kept encouraging me to keep moving, to keep running. Then I heard the loudest sound I had ever heard in my life. I didn't know what was happening at the time, but a bomb had exploded right next to us and I lost consciousness.

I don't know how long it was before I woke up. When I came to my senses, I wasn't looking for my mother; I was looking for my new friend. I was desperate to find her in the chaos all around me. People were bleeding and crying. Some were crawling. Some were writhing on the ground. I kept looking for my friend, calling out, "Where are you? Where are you?"

In my child's mind, I thought this was all happening because I hadn't run fast enough. I wanted to tell my friend that I was sorry and that I would run faster from now on. Perhaps you've had an experience like that, as a child or adult, where you mistakenly believed that it was your fault that things were falling apart all around you.

I ran frantically from person to person, searching for my friend. When I found her, she was lying completely still on the ground. She was bleeding all over, her body twisted at weird angles. I shook her and shook her, my heart aching as I cried, "Wake up, wake up, please wake up! I promise that I will run faster. Wake up!" Then I noticed that her arms were gone and her body was damaged beyond belief. She never woke up.

That was my life as a girl of five. I didn't play with toys. It was all about survival. I was fighting to live. I experienced war, suffering, fear, uncertainty, and loss. I had at last found a sweet friend and in the next moment I had lost her. All alone and terrified, I looked up at the sky and yelled at those strange hostile things flying in the air: "Why are you trying to kill me? I am just a little girl!"

All around me, I recognized the bodies of people from my village, many of them my aunts, uncles, and cousins who had always said, "You're bad luck, girl. Go play somewhere else!" Yet here they were on the ground, wounded or worse, and I was the one who was alive and unhurt. I remember thinking, "That's strange. They say I'm bad luck, but why are they hurt and bleeding while I'm standing here? I must be the one with really good luck."

I will never forget what I saw that day. It was one of those moments that seemed too terrible to be real. In the midst of all that horror, I made a decision deep within the core of my being that would forever change my life: *I will not run any longer. I will not hide.* From then on, no matter what would happen to me, I was going to take charge of my life. I knew in my heart that I had a purpose to fulfill and nothing was going to stop me.

That was the starting point of my determination to do whatever it took to confront and overcome any obstacle that came my way rather than run from it. I didn't know how I would stand up for myself, but I believed there had to be a way. Two years later, I began to discover that way.

Fighting for Your Dreams

Eventually, I was reunited with my family, and when the war was over I went to live with my grandparents. One blue-gray morning in Kimcheon, South Korea, I was awakened by a shout. Although the war had ended, sudden sounds still had an unsettling effect on me. Cautiously I slid open the rice paper window in the room. My uneasiness disappeared as I saw something that instantly captivated me.

There, in the early morning fog, my uncles were practicing an ancient martial art. I was mesmerized. The mists swirled with their fluid kicks. Their bodies glistened in the first light of dawn as they moved with amazing power and grace. What I saw awakened a deep feeling inside me. Their movements seemed mystical and yet so natural. To my seven-year-old mind, this was beautiful and exciting. It was important. Nothing had ever seemed so perfect. I had to learn how to do that myself. Little did I know how profoundly that moment would affect my life—and how much opposition I would face to fulfilling my desire.

As soon as I could, I asked my uncles to teach me how to do what they were doing, but they met my desire with laughter. "What?" they laughed. "You're supposed to learn how to cook and sew. And if you're lucky, someone will find you a husband." You see, being seven years old was not the obstacle. The obstacle was that I was a girl.

Teaching martial arts to little boys was not unusual. In fact, it was a common practice. Girls, however, were forbidden to learn martial arts. Why? Simply because it had been that way for centuries. Everyone told me it was silly for me to even imagine that my uncles or anybody else would teach me martial arts. I should look forward to growing up, getting married, and having twelve sons, they kept saying. But I didn't want to follow the path everyone expected of me. The women in my village were always working, working, working with their backs hunched over. That didn't seem like any fun to me. I didn't want to become like my mother. I didn't want to become like my grandmother. I didn't want to produce a lot of sons. I didn't want any of that. I knew in my heart that I was supposed to dedicate myself to learning martial arts.

No matter how often my uncles told me that it would be impossible for me to learn martial arts, I would not listen. I insisted that they teach me anyway. Finally one of my uncles came up with a strategy he thought would work. "Well," he said, "if we go ahead and give her lessons, she will probably give up." They were sure that I would stop being so persistent when I saw how difficult it was and started getting bruises from working out.

So every morning, I practiced. Yes, the work was hard and the bruises were many. I had to wear pants to hide the bruises so the other children wouldn't laugh at me. But to my uncles' surprise, I did not give up. To their further bewilderment, I progressed. I faced enormous difficulties—not in the art itself but in the continued resistance I met from those who believed that a woman couldn't and shouldn't be able to do that. I was, after all, breaking a five-thousand-year-old culture and tradition.

My family, my neighbors, and everyone I met applied enormous psychological and emotional pressure to try and stop me. My family even applied physical pressure, beating me and locking me in my room to keep me from practicing. My mother constantly nagged me and complained, "Why are you such a terrible daughter?" My father would come home drunk every night and beat my mother and me, demanding that I start acting like a marriageable young lady so he could have some peace in his life.

My mother was once so desperate to keep me from practicing that she took a pair of scissors and cut off my hair, leaving me with a short, funny-looking hairstyle. She wanted to make me feel so embarrassed that I would not want to leave the house to go practice. I cried, crawled into the corner, and touched my hair in disbelief. Then I thought to myself, "Okay, hair grows back. My hair will grow back. I will have to endure looking like this for a little while, but I am not going to let you stop me from doing what I love. You are not going to cut away my dreams. I will not give that power to you." In reality, the actions of my mother and family only made me more motivated and committed. The more I heard "No, no, no," the more I said to myself, "Yes, yes, yes. I can do it. I *will* do it."

When I tell this story, people always ask me whether I was upset with my family for trying to hold me down. Of course I shed a lot of tears and would become frustrated and angry. At some point, though, I realized that my mother was simply doing what she thought was right. She had been taught, as had her mother before her, that the best way to raise a little girl was to teach her to fulfill the role expected of her as a good wife and mother, not to encourage her to dream big. The people who raise us usually do what they think is best for us. If you can understand why they are acting the way they are, you can have greater compassion for them. That doesn't mean you have to accept their opinions or act like a victim. When you really want something that you believe in passionately, you can't let anyone rob you of your dreams.

Take a moment now and think about yourself. Have you ever had to stand up for yourself in the face of pressure from those who wanted to force you to live in a certain way? What sort of challenges are you facing now? What dreams are you fighting for?

The Spark That Ignites Your Flame

At this point in my life, I had an even worse reputation if that was possible. I was considered bad luck because I was born on the lunar new year as a girl instead of a boy, and now I was doing something that only boys and men were supposed to do. Everyone in my family was convinced that there was surely something wrong with me. While they would have been proud of my accomplishments had I been a boy, they regarded this as one more way that I was bringing shame upon them. In addition, my family was understandably worried that if I kept behaving in such odd ways, nobody would want to marry me and I would grow up to be a lonely, isolated, outcast old woman.

Still, my mind was set. I was determined to break out of the box everyone was trying to keep me trapped in. I knew I had to be true to the burning desire deep within. Although I didn't realize it at the time, that persistence is what would keep my dream alive through what was coming next.

One day I saw my grandfather talking to a strange woman in broad daylight, something that you would never normally see in our strict culture. All at once I realized what was happening—the woman was a matchmaker and my grandfather was bribing her to find me a husband. *That's not going to happen,* I told myself. I knew that I needed to find a way to make sure the matchmaker didn't like me, because if she did, I was going to be in big trouble.

When my grandfather asked me to serve tea to the two of them so the matchmaker could get a closer look at me, I knew this was my chance to thwart his plan. As I walked toward them holding the hot tea, I suddenly knocked the cup filled with steaming liquid onto the matchmaker's lap, making it look like an accident.

She was furious. "I don't care how much money you give me," she shouted. "She's bad luck and I'm never going to find her a husband. She is clumsy, she is no good, she is like a boy!" Other girls would have been dismayed that such an important person as a matchmaker didn't like them, but I was ecstatic.

As you can imagine, after I had spilled the tea on this woman, no other matchmaker would come anywhere near me. My family was at their wit's end. In their minds, they had done everything in their power to knock some sense into me. Now, they thought, if no one would marry me, they had only one choice left—to turn me over to the Buddhist monks and ask them to accept me as one of them.

That's how the only person who would come to believe in me entered my life. Following the painful episode with the matchmaker, my grandfather invited a monk to come to our house to talk over this plan with him. As they were talking, the monk kept glancing over at me. I had no idea why he was there, but I knew they must be talking about me. Then the monk motioned for me to come over to him. You may not realize how extremely unusual that was. In my culture at that time, girls were not allowed to even make eye contact with their elders. They always had to look down, and if they ever dared laugh or smile in the presence of a grown-up, they were supposed to cover their mouths. Girls were never allowed to speak directly to their grandfathers or even eat in the same room with them, nevertheless talk to a man who was a monk. That was like having a king ask me to talk with him.

I walked over to the monk, looking down at the ground. In a very gentle, amazingly kind voice, he asked, "So, little girl, don't you want to get married?"

"No, sir," I answered.

"But it's a woman's place to get married and be happy having sons and taking care of her family," he said.

"No, sir," I repeated. "That's not what I want."

"So what do you want to do when you grow up?"

"I want to become a teacher and help people."

What a bold statement that was. In the 1950s in Korea, it was unheard of for girls to have such dreams. I might as well have been saying, "I'm going to the moon."

"A teacher?" the monk asked. "What can you possibly teach?"

"I want to teach martial arts."

"Martial arts?"

"Yes, sir. I'm going to be the first woman teaching martial arts."

Unlike every other person in my life, he did not scoff at me or dismiss my audacious claim. Instead, in the same gentle tone he said, "Look at me."

Since girls were not allowed to look a monk in the eye, I thought he must be crazy. But he took his hand, put it under my chin, and lifted my head up. "Um hum," he said, as he studied my face for what seemed like an eternity. I had no idea what he was thinking. Then he looked directly into my eyes and said the words I had been waiting so long to hear: *"Yes, you will become a great teacher."*

I could not believe my ears. Someone was finally acknowledging me and my desires. Then he said something even more amazing: *"I will teach you."*

At first I didn't believe him. But when he again said, "I will teach you," I knew he was serious. For me, having someone of his stature say he was going to teach me martial arts was like winning a billion dollars in the lottery! It was the first time in my life that anyone had looked at me not as a lowly girl who was always disappointing everyone but as a human being who had value. In that split second, my life changed.

I was also starting to learn key lessons that would be reinforced many times in the years to come. I was learning that although we may feel as if everything is set against us and that the obstacles we face are insurmountable, that's not true. We cannot give up. We must hold on to our dreams. We must continue to do our part because the next big breakthrough is waiting to enter our lives at just the right moment. It didn't matter that no one else believed in me or liked me. I believed in myself, and now this great man believed in me. That was enough.

I was also learning another truth that has seen me through many a challenging time: you cannot and do not want to be liked by everyone. Wanting everyone to like you is not a good investment of your energy. Do you think Jesus or Buddha or the saints of East and West were welcomed and accepted by everyone? Do you think famous performers are liked by everybody? Does the fact that not everyone likes them make them a failure? Of course not. We all have different tastes and preferences. We're not all attracted to the same thing, and we don't need to be. The goal of life is not to convince every person you meet to like you. If you can connect heart to heart with those you are drawn to and with those who are drawn to you, that's what will lead you to your own brand of success.

When we stay true to ourselves and our desires, we magnetize to ourselves the people who will help us become all that we are meant to be. My teacher was the spark that ignited the flame in me. Who or what is the spark that has set you on fire? If you haven't experienced that yet, don't give up. Stay loyal to yourself and, in the depths of your heart, invite into your life those who are meant to be by your side. Remember that everything you are doing now is preparing you for that day. Stay true to your goals, especially when things seems hopeless. You must always believe in your own destiny and in your own dreams, for the saying "the darkest hour is just before the dawn" is so true.

The Doors That Open During Difficult Times

Once the monk made his astounding offer to teach me martial arts, my whole family was turned upside down and inside out. Not only was I breaking a five-thousand-year tradition prohibiting women from learning martial arts, but so was he by agreeing to teach me. When my family and the rest of the people in the village heard what the monk had promised, they thought he had literally gone mad. They abandoned him, refusing to allow him to enter their households or share in their food, as was the custom.

My teacher was forced to build his own makeshift hut outside the village because of his decision. It was there and in the nearby mountains that he taught me while I continued to live at home. I put everything I had into my training and into being the best I could be. I was extremely fortunate to have a gifted martial arts and ki energy master train me in unusual and unique ways from the time I was eight years old. He alone encouraged me to pursue my training. Day after day and year upon year, I learned things from him that opened my eyes to a world I never knew existed. As the years passed, I began to understand the deeper teachings and secrets of energy and martial arts that would eventually define what I teach today, including techniques of body, mind, and spirit and the seven steps to inner power I reveal here.

My teacher taught me about the ki energy, or life force, that is within all living things. He taught me that we can learn much from nature by closely observing its beauty and power. He showed me how to tap into and adapt the natural life force that is all around us, how to meditate, and how to generate and master energy. He taught me to commune with nature as well as with my own real nature and how to access my inner strength.

I would need every bit of inner strength I could muster in those years. Just because I had a teacher didn't mean my life was any easier. In many ways it became more difficult. I continued to be shamed and treated like an outcast. On top of that, every time I returned home after my training sessions, my mother would beat me. I made that part of my training. I would imagine that it wasn't her hitting me but a competitor or enemy. I would practice in my mind how to block the attacks, which strengthened me mentally. Whenever things got ugly in my life, I used every mental technique I was learning from my teacher to conquer and rise above those outer conditions. All the while, I was becoming proficient in my art and honing my skills. After many years of training under my master, a new path unexpectedly opened. It was born of a terrible tragedy and was one of the most difficult times in my life.

Every night my father would come home to our one-room house drunk. At night, it was as if he had turned into another person. The sound of his footsteps coming into the house would fill my mother, me, and my younger brother with fear. There was nowhere to hide from my father's tirades. Not long after we would place before him the food he demanded to be served, he would find something wrong with it. Soon it was as if a bomb were exploding. He would overturn the table, smashing it and everything on it to the floor. Then he would start hitting and kicking me and sometimes my mother as he shouted at me and blamed me for whatever was going wrong in his life.

This continued for years, until I was in my early twenties. The only person who showed me love during this time, besides my teacher, was my brother. During one of my father's particularly violent outbursts, my brother couldn't watch my father abuse me any longer. He stepped between me and my father's punches, and when my father started kicking and punching him, my tall, strong brother instinctively did the unthinkable. He hit my father back. For a child to hit a parent, even in situations like this, was a very serious and shameful offense. It was unforgivable.

The next day, I found a letter from my brother. "Dear Sister," he wrote. "Not everyone loves wild daisies. Not everyone notices them or cares for them like they do the roses or the lilies. You are like a wild daisy. No one recognizes you, but I recognize you for who you are. You are windblown. You sway but do not break. I am not strong like you are, but please have a share of my life and live for me too." The moment I read his heartfelt note, I knew something was wrong. I searched everywhere for him, but I couldn't find him. Because he used to call me "wild daisy," I decided to run to a nearby field where many yellow flowers and wild daisies grew. That's where I found him, lying there. I shook him over and over and called his name, but he never moved.

My brother's guilt and remorse at having hit my father was so deep that he took his own life. In our culture, if a young man committed suicide, it was considered an overwhelming disgrace for the entire family. With this new stigma and humiliation hanging over our heads, we had to leave the village before the entire family was cast out. Grandfather decided we would all go to America.

When I told my master about what had happened and my grandfather's plan, he said, "This is a sign. It's time for you to go." It was heart-wrenching to hear him say that. I didn't want to leave because I had become very attached to my teacher. Yet he knew that this was the next step on my journey, that it was the only way I would be able to pass on what I had learned from him and fulfill my dream of becoming a martial arts teacher. "If you don't go," he finally had to tell me, "you will be insulting me."

So at twenty-three, I suddenly found myself in an entirely different country and culture. I lived with my family in Vermont in a trailer park. None of us knew how to speak or read or write a word of English. I didn't know how to drive, I didn't dress like other people, I had no money, and I was—and still am—only 4'11". From my first days in this new world, I never lost sight of my dream to become a martial arts teacher. But I had to tend to first things first. Our family had only $300 between us, so I needed to find a job.

I had just arrived from a foreign country. What could I do? One thing I knew how to do was clean, so at first the only jobs I could get were cleaning bathrooms at a Howard Johnson hotel and pumping gas, which I was happy to do. I was very proud of my cleaning job. Today when people ask me, "When did you feel you had your first success in your life?" I respond, "When I was cleaning the toilets on my first job." I'm not ashamed of that. In Korea, I was cleaning the house and the toilet and getting beaten. Here, I was cleaning and getting paid for it! I felt like a millionaire. This job was my first step in creating my new life.

Nevertheless, we faced many challenges in those early days, and I had to remind myself to put into practice everything my master had taught me. You can imagine how difficult it was at first, not knowing anything about American culture and having an Asian face. People made fun of me and called me all sorts of insulting names. In the beginning that bothered me because I didn't understand why they would do that. Then I said to myself, "Wait a minute. Why am I letting them bother me? They really don't know what I am like or what I have to offer. They are making a judgment based on their own limited information. That's what they are using to judge me. I'm the one who is stupid if I let that bother me."

I told myself that I would not let their ignorance rob me of my joy, my happiness, or my success. I gave myself permission to be patient and trust that when the time came, I would have an opportunity to show people the real me and find the individuals I was meant to be with and teach martial arts to. At the same time, I knew that if I was sitting at home, nobody would come knocking on my door. We all have goals and dreams, but we have to be the ones to take action to make them a reality.

Overcoming in Every Aspect of Your Life

As I scrubbed the toilets and sinks at work and went about my daily activities, I was constantly looking for an opening where I could begin to offer my talents. I visualized my future plans and saw myself teaching students. In my heart, I wanted to be the spark that would light a flame in others, as my master had done for me. Every day as I walked to and from my home, I would pass a high school and watch the students coming and going. They behaved differently from the children in my village in Korea in so many ways, not the least of which was that boys and girls were allowed to attend classes together. I realized that I could teach these students so much. But how could I get started? I looked like one of the students myself. I had long hair, weighed about ninety pounds, and wasn't used to wearing makeup or high heels.

A plan began to form in my mind. I decided to sit outside the principal's office and wait for my opportunity to explain what I wanted to do. I expected that somebody would ask me, "What do you want? Who are you? What is your name?" I would get out my Korean-English dictionary and practice my answers: "I would like to teach martial arts. My name is Tae Yun Kim." I imagined the other questions they would ask and how I would answer them. For a full month I sat outside the office for several hours each day, waiting to get the opportunity to show what I could do. Finally, I was invited in and got my chance. I learned an important lesson during this time: never give up. So many times in life, we want to give up just before we are about to succeed. But if we are persistent and consistent, doors will open.

As I expected, the administrators asked me questions. I didn't understand everything they were saying, but I understood their quizzical expressions.

"I would like to teach martial arts," I told them.

"Oh no, we don't want martial arts," they replied. "Besides, we don't have the money to hire you."

I told them I didn't want any money and that I wanted to volunteer. I smiled and was very confident.

They asked me how I could teach if I couldn't speak English. Well, I was ready for that question too.

"Correct," I said. "And you don't speak Korean. I learn fast. I can teach martial arts in broken English." Bruce Lee was very popular at the time and, sure enough, they brought up another point I had anticipated: "We don't want our students to get hurt or break a kneecap—their own or someone else's." I had already prepared my answer with the help of the dictionary: "No, no," I replied in my broken English. "I'm going to teach them how to break through their mental barriers. I'm going to teach them confidence and discipline and how to stay focused and be positive."

The administrators had their doubts, but when they heard that, they gave me a chance. Many students as well as teachers would gather each day to watch the strange and fascinating movements, routines, and lessons I was teaching. Amazingly, the troublemakers started to become better students. Within months, my class had become the most popular in the school. Even more amazing, I was voted Teacher of the Year and given an award. The administrators were so pleased that they let me use the small gymnasium at the elementary school to teach martial arts classes to the teachers and parents who now wanted to take lessons themselves. I was putting into practice the life principles my teacher had taught me and they were working.

As time went on, I was always looking for ways to expand my reach. After many months, I was able to open a martial arts "studio" in an old garage. I taught martial arts classes after school, at midnight I would go off to do my janitorial work at the hotel, and during weekends I would pump gas.

Four years went by, and I had at last saved enough money to open a school where I could teach martial arts and pass on the life skills and wisdom my teacher had instilled in me. At the end of every class, the students and I would shout out the affirmation that would become my motto: *"He can do, she can do, why not me?"*

One opportunity led to another. As news of my successful high school physical education class spread, I received an offer from the University of Vermont in Burlington to teach an accredited phys ed class, which in turn led to a teaching assignment at IBM. I also worked hard for years to make women's divisions for Tae Kwon Do competitions more fair in a largely male-dominated sport. In 1978, I accomplished a big dream of mine. As head coach, I led the first-ever U.S. women's Tae Kwon Do team at the Pre-World Games in Seoul, South Korea, where the team won a gold medal as well as several other metals. This helped pave the way for women to compete in martial arts in the Olympics, and I have since coached other athletes as well.

Eventually, I went on to develop my own branch of martial arts, naming it Jung SuWon, and in 1989 I founded the Jung SuWon Academy. You may wonder why I founded my own school of martial arts. Tae Kwon Do and other martial arts schools were being marketed more and more as a sport. Martial arts was even becoming an Olympic sport. The martial arts teachers I observed were all emphasizing the techniques—kick, kick, kick, kick, punch,

punch, punch, punch. That emphasis on technique, however, didn't convey the centuries-old tradition at the heart of martial arts that focused on how to develop one's inner power and full potential.

I knew that real martial arts was not simply learning to do a series of repetitive moves, kicks, and punches so one could compete in tournaments and have instant gratification and glory. The true way of the martial arts warrior is much more than overcoming in combat. It is overcoming in every aspect of daily living. If you're honest, don't many aspects of your life feel like you're in a battle? We fight to meet our financial obligations, to keep our jobs and provide for our families, to maintain good health and good relationships, to stay centered in the midst of day-to-day stresses. At the heart of the martial arts I teach is training to overcome in the mental, emotional, and spiritual battlegrounds of everyday life.

I felt I would be betraying my master if I didn't preserve and pass on the inner tradition at the heart of his teaching. I decided that the only way to do that was to create a branch of martial arts that reflected the fundamental principle of unifying body, mind, and spirit as one. Thus, Jung SuWon was born.

I have had my share of ordeals, of course, both professional and personal, but I have been determined to learn from each one. The art of Jung SuWon has never failed to help me confront any difficulty or attain any goal I've set my mind to, and it hasn't failed those I've taught. Over the years I have counseled and coached people from all walks of life and from all over the world to incorporate those same principles into their own lives—from troubled teenagers, gang members, abused women, and young people on the verge of suicide to Olympic teams, corporate executives, and entrepreneurs.

As an essential step in that process, they have learned what you'll learn here—to become aware of the power of their real self and to listen to an ever-present consciousness within, which I call the "Silent Master." Your Silent Master is, in reality, your original self, your real self. Though you have not used that term, you've probably already experienced your Silent Master as that "inner voice" of intuition and inspiration that has guided you at key points on your life's journey. In the chapters that follow, you'll come to understand more about your original self and how to tap into its strength, joy, and power to realize greater and greater possibilities in your life.

I've always believed that if this person or that person can do something, why not me and why not you? If I fail, I'll try again. And again. This takes effort, but has anything worthwhile ever been accomplished without effort? Even if something has never been done before, why should that stop us?

Others said it was impossible for me to even think about learning martial arts in the face of a five-thousand-year-old culture forbidding women to do that. They said it was impossible when I, a woman, attained a black belt in my martial art. Then (more impossible) that I, a woman, could become a female martial arts master. And then (absolutely impossible!) that I could become a female grandmaster. Well, so much for what is supposedly impossible. I want to be clear, though—there's a difference between aiming for what you know in your heart is possible and indulging in daydreaming or impossible fantasies that are not real goals. You'll learn more about being realistic *and* aiming high with determination later on.

People sometimes say that the path to a goal seems too long, so they don't want to even bother starting. Yet if you take one step on that journey, you've just shortened it. Journeys are not accomplished without a map, however. That's why I decided to write this book. You can learn how to apply the life secrets and seven steps to inner power that were handed down to me and that I teach my students so that you, too, can break through to awesome and become the master of your own life. The art of Jung SuWon is the art of living your life with power, purpose, and passion. When you learn this art, I guarantee you, there will be no obstacle you cannot overcome.

FOR YOUR REFLECTION

I invite you to use the questions at the end of each chapter to help you reflect on and incorporate into your life the concepts you are learning in this book. You may want to devote a special notebook to answering these questions and journaling about what you are discovering. There are no right or wrong answers. Your journey and the things you discover along the way are your own. The questions and exercises are intended to stimulate in you a greater awareness and appreciation of your true self, that quiet voice of wisdom within you.

1. Have you ever seen a blade of grass growing through cement or a small tree growing through solid rock? If you look carefully, you'll see that it is the cement or rock that has cracked.

• What obstacles in your life right now feel like rocks weighing you down? Keep these in mind as you work through the exercises in this book. The purpose of this book is to help you break through those obstacles.

2. Write down the three things you most want to accomplish in life. Do not limit yourself to what others have said is possible or not possible for you to achieve. Be honest with yourself and aim for awesome.

• Which of the three things you wrote down is the most important to you? Why?

Chapter Two

Who Am I?

Who am I? If I asked you to answer that question right now, what would you say? Would you say something like "I'm a graphic designer," "I'm a nurse," "I'm an executive," "I'm a student," "I'm a father," "I'm a mother"? Or would you say something that describes your abilities or character, such as "I'm an athlete," "I'm an optimist," or "I'm a worrier"? We tend to describe ourselves by our career, our roles in life, or the positive or negative personality traits we've developed over the years and accepted as being "us." But is that who you really are? In actuality, you may only have a partial idea of the real you and the enormous creative power that resides within you.

Asking and seeking the answer to "Who am I?" is not as easy as it may seem, but it is absolutely essential if you wish to express your fullest potential in life. The reason it requires effort is that from the time you were born, the people around you have been feeding you their opinions, their advice, their ideas about who you are and the direction you should go in. That information may have little or nothing to do with the truth of who you really are, your original essence. Yet all that chatter has become mixed in with your concept of who you think you are, influencing what you dared dream of achieving. If you are honest, today you may even be following a lifestyle you inherited from your parents or mentors, your culture or society without ever realizing that you had a choice to take a different path.

The truth is, you are exactly where you are today because of the way you have answered the question "Who am I?" Why? Because how you answer that question determines what choices you make for yourself moment by moment every day of your life. You choose only what you believe is possible to choose, and those choices determine what you do with your life and who you become. If you believe you are shy, for instance, you will not choose to become a performer, even if you have the talent and inner desire to be a performer. If you believe you aren't a good student, you may never choose a course of study that could lead you to the career you would really like to have.

It is essential, then, to know the real truth about yourself and your capabilities. The purpose of this book is to show you that you may have made limited choices based on limited information about yourself. It's time to take another look. It's time to start making choices based on a more complete knowledge of who you *really* are.

In today's world, where the answers to almost everything are at your fingertips, "Who am I?" is one question you won't find a quick answer to by searching on Google. Your GPS won't instantly point you in the right direction. You have to dive into yourself at the deepest level and do some soul searching to find and experience the truth. Just as you cannot see below the surface of choppy seas or muddy water, so you can only see deeply into your own self when you create a calm and quiet space. I want to help you do that here so you can experience the creative power of your original self—the power that will propel you toward your goals.

Ask yourself: What do I want to become? Have I realized my dreams and goals? Do I have the career I want, the relationships I want? Do I like who I am? Am I happy or am I just making believe that I am? If a doctor were to tell me that I had only one month to live, would I be able to truthfully say with all my heart, "Yes, I am content with my life"?

If you are satisfied with your life at this moment, those questions may hold no interest for you right now. If, on the other hand, you find yourself holding dreams that feel so true yet seem out of reach, if you are unfulfilled, frustrated, alienated, empty, if you still have a yearning to realize a deeper sense of joy, peace, and purpose, or if there is simply more you want to accomplish, it is time to extend your vision of who you are. No matter who you are, no matter what obstacles and limitations you face at this moment, you can change your life and your state of mind completely. *You can decide who you want to become.*

Awakening to the Powerful Presence Within

Waiting quietly within you is a presence, a force, a state of consciousness that gives you the power to overcome mental and physical limitations in your life, the power to harmonize and change discordant situations, the power to create and to achieve goals. It gives you the power to experience peace and joy regardless of the circumstances around you—the power to be who you really are. In Jung SuWon, we refer to this presence within as the Silent Master or Silent Master consciousness.

When you tap into the consciousness of the Silent Master within, you begin to take control of your life. You may have been drifting through life before; now you are driving through life and toward your goals. You experience a new sense of freedom, creativity, purpose, and peace of mind. You find yourself glad to be alive every day for the sheer pleasure of experiencing life—of experiencing yourself.

The keys from the art of Jung SuWon that you'll explore here will help you awaken to this powerful presence within and empower you to recognize and express the qualities of your Silent Master in your daily life. As you open to your true potential in this way, you'll discover more of your beauty, your strength, and your courage.

At the core of the philosophy I teach are six truths about your Silent Master. I call them "Silent Master images" and you'll understand why when you read the section on visualization, or, as I call it, "future memory." In essence, these images describe who you truly are and the awesome power you have within you now to shape your life. As you move through this book, you'll learn much more about these foundational concepts and how to put them into action in your life. Here I'll simply touch on these truths to give you a brief introduction to them. For now, think of each one as a seed-thought designed to blossom into a practical understanding of your true being and power as you contemplate "Who am I?" Give yourself complete freedom and permission to fall in love with who you are and who you are becoming.

SIX SILENT MASTER IMAGES

You are one of a kind

Your Silent Master is your real self, *your original self. It expresses itself through your thinking, through true ideas and thoughts in your mind. It is your eternal Selfhood that exists apart from your brain (which is a sensory processor only) and the personality traits imposed on you from your environment.*

I cannot emphasize enough how important it is to live by the truth that you are one of a kind. As a child in training under my martial arts master, I would be in tears as I told him how my family was treating me—how they were pounding negative messages into my ears every day, telling me I was no good, I was bad luck, I was a tomboy, I was a curse, I was a disaster, I was never going to be happy, I could never be a martial artist and I was crazy to even think like that.

No matter how much I wanted to get angry and fight when I heard those words, my master would say to me: "Just remember: *You are one of a kind.* You are not your mother and you are not your grandmother. Do not let their opinions or judgments or ideas affect who you can be, because you are not them. You are unique. Your mother has copied her lifestyle from your grandmother, as she was taught to do. You say you want to become a practitioner of the martial arts—even a teacher. No woman has ever done that. So you need to accept that you are one of a kind and acknowledge it. *You* need to believe that's who you are before you can convince anyone else." He encouraged me to affirm that truth over and over.

Now it is my turn to tell you: I know who you are. Now *you* have to know who you are. *You are one of a kind.* You are not just someone's son or daughter, brother or sister, mother or father. You're not just an employee or manager at such and such a company. We've all heard about people who lose their job or break up with their boyfriend or girlfriend and then lash out violently at others or even want to commit suicide because they believe their life is now finished. Have you ever felt that way yourself? Remember, your job, your relationships, what other people say about you is *not* who you are. If someone doesn't appreciate who you are, you are still one of a kind with unlimited opportunity and potential. No one can take that away from you—unless you allow them to.

Do you need proof that you are unique, that you are one of a kind? Turn your hands so your palms are facing up. Now look at your thumbs. Today we have technology so advanced that we can make 3-D copies of objects, transplant organs and stem cells, clone some species of animals. The one thing no one can copy and that makes you uniquely you is your thumbprint. No one else in the world has your thumbprint. Even identical twins who are born only seconds apart and who look exactly alike do not have the same thumbprint. Your thumbprint is entirely unique to you.

Knowing that you are one of a kind means that you can't compare yourself to anyone else. A grape is a grape, not a tangerine. An eagle is meant to be an eagle and cannot be compared to a tiger. A daisy never asks itself, "Why aren't I a rose?" Each of these creations has their own beauty and their own strength. You, too, have your own beauty and your own strength. So don't ever say to yourself, "Why aren't I like him or her?"

You might not realize how much you compare yourself to others. It can happen in obvious or subtle ways, both of which can end up making you feel "less than" someone else when you are simply "different from" them. Without being conscious of it, we compare ourselves to others in all sorts of settings—in business dealings or when we compete with co-workers, when interacting with friends or neighbors, at school or when playing sports, when we are waiting with others in a long line at the cash register, or even when we flip through a magazine or watch TV.

I remember when one of my Jung SuWon students would point to another student who was good at running and jumping and say to me, "I really want to be like him. Look how he jumps and kicks! It's like he's flying through the air. I can't wait to be able to do that." That student was very talented himself, but I knew that jumps, which require a student to be lighter, smaller, and faster, would not be his specialty. Some people are built for speed, and they can run and jump quickly. Others generate power from their firm stances on the ground. With this student's physique, I could see that he would excel at techniques on the ground, where students kick or punch from standing positions without jumping for height or distance. Those types of movements are no better or worse than running and jumping techniques; they are just different.

I would explain to this student that everyone is built differently, and therefore each individual excels at different types of activities. Each person has his or her own special talents and reason for being, as does every part of nature. It wouldn't work if an eagle tried to be a tiger, would it? I reminded him, as I remind all my students: You are one of a kind. If you keep comparing yourself to others, you will miss the opportunity to discover and develop your own best qualities and strengths. Whatever you are doing in your life, discover what you are best at and strive to be the best *you* can be.

You and the life force are one

Your Silent Master consciousness was born out of the infinite life force creating and animating the universe. You exist as a part of the universe; therefore, the life force is what creates and animates you. It is the power that beats your heart. Because you are this consciousness, whatever qualities the life force possesses, you possess also.

Your Silent Master is the part of you that is connected to the same creative life force that made the universe. Your Silent Master, or Silent Master consciousness, is therefore the expression I use to describe the original, pure life force as it exists within you personally. Over thousands of years, different traditions have called this universal creative energy or life force by different names.

To be clear, I am not speaking from a "religious" point of view when I use the term *life force*. I'm talking about the natural, universal force—a spiritual force, if you will—that underlies all of nature. In Eastern traditions this force is known as ki (pronounced "key"), chi, or prana. Ki in its pure, original form is the life force, the energy, that creates life and sets everything in motion: the swirling of galaxies, the birth of stars, the hatching of an eagle's egg, the delicate unfolding of a flower's petals, the infant growing into an adult. All those activities are evidence of universal ki energy manifesting as life and motion.

How do eagles know they must go find food to feed their eaglets? How do young birds know when it's time to spread their wings and fly? How do salmon know when it's time to make their incredible journey upstream to their birthplace to lay their eggs? How does a newborn child know to open its mouth to be fed? How does that same child know when it's time to crawl and time to walk? No one has taught her these things. She just knows them. At one with the life force, those behaviors come naturally.

We look in awe at the majesty and power that expresses itself through nature, but we don't realize that we are endowed with the same awe-inspiring life force and energy. The pure, original ki that created the universe is within you right now too.

At one time or another, you have probably felt that animating life force; you just haven't called it that. Often we become aware of that energy only when we act suddenly and instinctively in the midst of a life-and-death crisis—when we have to move quickly against all odds to lift a heavy object to save someone's life, for example. Or we may become aware of that force welling up within us when we follow a strong prompting to do something completely outside our normal routine, only to find that doing so kept us out of danger. Perhaps you can recall an experience where you unconsciously tapped into a powerful energy far beyond your ordinary expectations. You may have marveled afterwards and said to yourself, "Wow, how did I do that?" Maybe you decided your performance was a fluke. It was not a fluke; it was evidence of the inner power we all possess—ki power.

All of us, then, are born with a specific purpose to fulfill, and we already possess the potential to fulfill it because, as the Silent Master image above says, "whatever qualities the life force possesses, you possess also." This inner power is at your disposal twenty-four hours a day, seven days a week. You simply have to relearn how to access it, cultivate it, and put it into effective action in your life.

I remember when the idea of the life force stopped being theoretical for me and became something real and tangible. After some years of martial arts training, one cold winter day my master said to me, "Now it's time to see what you've really learned about mastering ki energy by putting what you've learned into practice." I was still quite young at the time. He took me to a frozen pond and showed me a spot where the ice had not yet frozen over. He asked me to practice what he had taught me about ki by climbing into the water and generating enough ki to warm myself.

At first, I thought he was crazy. How did he expect me to get into freezing cold water? Yet I knew that he would not ask me to do something he did not think I was capable of doing. So I dipped my toes into the pond. Sure enough, the water was unbelievably cold. Still, I did as he asked and submerged my body. Then with great concentration, I applied what he had taught me. My body became so hot that the cold no longer had any control over me.

"Why can't we naturally do things like that?" you may wonder. "If we are indeed one with the life force that is behind the whole universe, why don't we feel more energetic? Why are we tired, why can't we accomplish what we want to, why do our goals seem to elude us?" The answer is that our own negative thoughts, attitudes, and emotions act like filters that keep this mighty river of energy down to a trickling stream. One purpose of the Jung SuWon principles I teach and that I will share with you here is to learn how to purify this filter—to purify your thinking and feeling so that energy flows more freely and powerfully, enabling you to access your inner power in creative and effective ways.

Your thoughts create reality

Your Silent Master consciousness knows itself to be immaterial in substance, but it also takes form as your physical body and the material world around you. Thus, you may describe yourself as being both immaterial (spiritual) and material (physical) at the same time.

Isn't it true that most of the time we focus our thoughts and attention on our physical self and our physical life? Yet our physical self is just one part of our total energy field. We are both physical *and* spiritual beings.

Thinking about a spiritual self that seems to be outside the concerns of your physical life may seem impractical and unrealistic. However, once you understand that this spiritual part of yourself is intimately involved in the life you create day by day, you will start to see and act differently. The immaterial aspect of yourself, your spiritual being, is what provides the real energy behind any physical manifestation in life—driving it, creating it, sustaining it.

When you mentally conceive, you set your creative process in motion. That's because what you conceive, or perceive, is the starting point for all your decisions, actions, responses, judgments, and attitudes. Directly or indirectly, all those activities, help create your self-concept, your body, and the environment around you. Our thoughts and feelings are, in essence, pure energy. Whatever we think about consciously and subconsciously manifests in our daily life in one form or another. That applies to all the negative, self-limiting, and doubting thoughts that hold us back as well as the confident, determined, supportive thoughts that propel us into positive action.

Say you have a great desire to achieve a certain goal, but part of you also believes that you aren't good enough to attain that goal or you really don't deserve it. Those negative thoughts are like a dam, blocking the energy you're pumping into achieving your goal. Or perhaps someone convinced you that achieving your goal would be impossible for anyone to do. Have you ever experienced a situation like that, where you were enthusiastic about a new idea, but you allowed another person's criticism or cynicism to suck the life right out of your dreams and plans?

As I noted before, we do have to be realistic and set achievable goals. What I'm talking about here, though, is understanding that negative thinking can deflate the true and inspiring ideas that come from your real self. Fear and self-doubt can become your own worst enemies.

It takes vigilance to examine and reexamine the thoughts that run through your mind, the inner dialogue that may come from beliefs that were originally planted in you a long time ago, telling you again and again, "You cannot do that." In the next chapter you'll learn some techniques you can use to free yourself from negative thinking and instead create strong habits of right thinking that will boost your creativity, determination, and drive.

You are creative energy

Your Silent Master knows itself as the source of mental, emotional, and material energy—your energy, which you are free to utilize and control in creating what you desire. Therefore, you are a co-creator, cooperating with the life force of the universe to shape yourself and the world around you.

This Silent Master image reinforces the truth that you are a co-creator of your world. You are in charge of directing your energy to manifest your deepest and truest desires. As a co-creator, keep in mind that you can also use your energy to create the life you *don't* want though the choices you make.

Everything is a manifestation of some form of energy, positive or negative. I said earlier that you are exactly where you are today because of the way you have answered the question "Who am I?" Another way of saying that is that the picture of your body, your environment, and your life right now is a result of how you have directed your energy, your life force, up to now. The picture of your life that you see right now didn't exist until it was transformed into that picture. And if you choose, you can transform it again.

Many people have resigned themselves to feeling that they don't have any control over their environment, so why bother caring one way or another what happens. They wake up, go to work, come home, go to bed, and start all over again without any real direction or understanding that they do, in fact, have tremendous control over their lives—that they possess creative energy and are therefore co-creators of their worlds. By accepting things as they are, they are choosing to pour their energy into a mold of helplessness rather than into a more positive scenario.

Don't ever feel helpless. No matter what environment you are in, there is always room to be creative in making positive changes and improving your circumstances. If you have a job in sales, perhaps your next creative move is to do what it takes to become the star sales person on your team. Maybe your next step is to qualify to become a manager in your department or train for a different position. Be willing to commit to and do the work required for that next step as "a co-creator, cooperating with the life force of the universe to shape yourself and the world around you."

Keep in mind, too, that success is different for everyone. We don't all have to become a Bill Gates. Success comes as you use your creative energy in your everyday environment to do one thing after another that makes a difference. Most people wouldn't want to have a job cleaning toilets, but when I took that as my first job when I came to the United States, I knew it was only a stepping-stone toward fulfilling my dream of teaching martial arts.

When you truly comprehend that you are a co-creator and not just a receiver, you don't limit yourself by accepting someone else's rules of how life should unfold for you. You've already heard about some of the challenges I've had to face and overcome, but I also carry this kind of thinking into my everyday life. If I receive an invitation to an event that says, "You can bring one person with you," but I want to bring a second person along, I say, "I'm going to ask if it's possible for two people to come with me." I'm not losing anything by asking. If they say yes, great. But many people won't even think of asking when they see those "rules" in print in front of them.

If I'm headed to a store to purchase something I urgently need, but because of bad traffic I get there as the owner is putting up the "closed" sign, I don't shrug my shoulders and walk away. I knock. Why not? Again, I won't lose anything by trying. In fact, what usually happens is that when the owner comes to the door, I politely explain that I just need one item and I know exactly what it is. The next thing I know, the door is opening. Not only that, I have an opportunity to meet the store owner and we become great friends.

Amazing things can happen if you are willing to step outside the lines you draw in your own mind. Those are minor examples, but just think what you can accomplish when you take charge, see yourself as a co-creator of every circumstance in your life, and work hand in hand with the universe and your Silent Master to become the director of your life.

You have the power to fulfill your dreams

Your Silent Master is completely aware, infinitely intelligent, and ready to give you all the insight, information, and direction you need to fulfill your dreams, ambitions, and goals. In fact, this consciousness is the source of all your true desires.

Your truth is already within you. You are responsible for bringing it forth. You can do this by listening to and following through on the inclinations that are your own. Your Silent Master always knows the best course for you to take and is constantly talking to you by giving you thoughts and inclinations that are accompanied by a feeling of rightness. We call this "intuition." Intuition is not something mysterious but a normal, natural way of hearing the right direction voiced by your Silent Master.

On your life journey, your Silent Master will bring you exactly what you need each step of the way. My Silent Master gave me desire and determination. It gave me feelings of self-acceptance and perseverance to carry out my desires. It brought me into contact with my martial arts teacher at a crucial turning point in my life. It gave me direction on what decisions to make and the path I should take. I had to choose, as you will, to listen to that part of myself rather than the loud, critical voices around me. I wasn't always a grandmaster. I was a frightened girl, and I had plenty of opportunities to make all kinds of excuses for not rising above my environment. But I made the personal decision not to accept those limitations. I chose to remain true to myself.

It wasn't easy, of course. I had to summon all the determination I could. I had to determine not to let anyone rob me of my dreams, clip my wings, or hold me down. I had to determine to rise up, like a phoenix rises from the ashes to be reborn. As a young girl and later a young woman, it would have been nice to have the loving support of family and friends as I worked toward my goals instead of being laughed at, ostracized, and even beaten like a dog at times. What I discovered, though, is that even in the worst situations, I had a choice. Even if my choices were limited, I could do something that would move me a little closer to my goals.

Why is it that some people rise above the ugly circumstances around them and others are trampled by them? Those who ultimately overcome are those who bring forward all their desire, all their passion, all their determination and belief in themselves. The desire to achieve your goals has to be stronger than the self-doubt, the criticism, and the abuse. When you believe that you don't have the power to fulfill your dreams or that the next hurdle in front of you is impossible to overcome, you are the one who is beating yourself into submission. In the face of any challenge or obstacle, know that your real self is there to guide you forward. The power of your real self is strong enough to love and support you through any situation.

You are complete, peaceful, and fulfilled

Your Silent Master expresses completeness, fulfillment, harmony, peace, joy, and love and imparts these qualities to everything it creates.

Aren't fulfillment, peace, joy, and love what we are all striving for when we get right down to it? What more can we ask for?

"Well," you might say, "to be honest, I want more than that. I need money to take care of myself and my family. I need a good career, a nice house, and a big car to feel secure and at peace." That's perfectly fine if that's your definition of peace and fulfillment. You alone can determine what will make you happy. No one else can do that for you. You may be happy earning $30,000 a year while others are happy only when they are earning a million dollars a year. You might need a seven-bedroom house to feel happy while someone else is fine living in a three-room apartment. Only you will know.

What the Silent Master image above tells us is that, whatever goals you have that are appropriate for you, you can work with your Silent Master to achieve them. Since you and your Silent Master are one, you have the same qualities it has and therefore you can access and express those qualities to fulfill your life's plan. For instance, since your Silent Master energy is creative, you are creative and can express that creativity in how you choose to shape your life and your environment. With your Silent Master's joy, you can be grateful for the blessings in your life, express gratitude to others, and experience unconditional happiness. With your Silent Master's love, you can appreciate your unique gifts and one-of-a-kind individuality and give yourself the love and care you need. With your Silent Master's power, you can determine to be proactive instead of simply reacting to events and circumstances as if you are a victim.

Your Silent Master consciousness is within you now, energizing your body, mind, and spirit with the life force. You can allow your pure Silent Master energy to shine through everything you do when you choose to think as your real self would think, feel as your real self would feel, and act as your real self would act.

The Pressure to Be Something You Are Not

The six Silent Master images reflect your true essence and the power that exists within you. Before you explore how you can begin to unlock this power, it's important to consider why the Silent Master is so named. Why is it "silent"? If all this power and dominion are available, why isn't it automatically out there healing you and your problems, making you the strong, successful, achieving person you want to be? Where has the Silent Master been all these years?

The Silent Master has always been there. It is silent only when we are not aware of it, when we do not focus on it, when we do not identify it as our real self. It is silent out of neglect—our neglect. It takes effort to listen to that which is silent, but when you make the decision to find your Silent Master, its power begins to unfold. That power unfolds to the degree you strive to open yourself to receive it.

So the real question is not "Where has my Silent Master been all these years?" The question is "Where have *you* been?" To answer that question, let's look in more detail at the idea I touched on at the beginning of this chapter—the influence of our surroundings in shaping the concept we have of ourselves.

Isn't it interesting that we call our beginning a "conception"? We were "conceived" by our parents. Truly, from the day we were born, we have been in the business of forming concepts about ourselves. Perhaps one of the first concepts you formed was that you were dependent. All the care, nourishment, and attention you received came from outside yourself, from your immediate environment—most likely first from your parents and then from school, work, and social environments. Because you were dependent on others, those who were first responsible for your care began to shape your identity according to their beliefs and expectations. How? Primarily by telling you what was "good" and what was "bad." Many things they taught you benefited you. As a young, dependent child, it was usually to your advantage to learn from the people who were taking care of you. In most cases, they had your best interests at heart. Yet many things you took as fact were only their opinions.

No one had to teach you to cry, to smile, to laugh, or to feel hunger and thirst, pain and pleasure. Even those automatic behaviors, though, were conditioned by the pressures of approval and disapproval by peers and authority figures. So you possibly learned to hide, avoid, or distort your natural impulses, impulses that were designed to help you know yourself.

Because of your dependency in your formative years, the pressure to conform to group standards outside yourself was enormous. As a child you couldn't alienate the people who were responsible for your physical and emotional survival, so you went along with them the best you could. Perhaps you resisted certain concepts about yourself along the way, but for the most part you accepted what others had to say about you and acted accordingly. Why shouldn't you? Conformity was meant to be a good thing, something that would allow you to adjust and get along with the world with minimum conflict.

As you continued to interact with your environment, you learned how to act to avoid conflict, to avoid the displeasure of authority figures, and to secure praise and pleasure. You may have learned that the path of least resistance was to do what was expected of you, do what you were told, not be too different, and not argue with the system. Although the system was designed to give you a share of safety and security, it did not guarantee happiness or fulfillment or freedom—or any of the things that make life truly worth living.

This system of socialization means that we start creating a personal "brand" of who we are based on how others made us feel—not just family members, but also teachers, those we looked up to, those we played with, those who may have bullied us or become our best friends. Their feedback could make you feel that you were not smart enough or that you were a budding Einstein, that you were clumsy or the next Olympic star, that you were boring or creative, and on and on. By the time you reach the point where you are ready to depend only on yourself, you are not automatically free from those prior influences. The programming is usually set. The person you are is, to a larger or lesser degree, the person others taught you to be.

How many choices have you made, even your most important choices, such as choosing a career or a spouse, that were really based on someone else's ideas and preferred choices for you? Even some of your good beliefs may not reflect your true being. For example, a person who has become a successful lawyer may have been thwarted from expressing his true love for designing cars. When this happens, as it does to many people, you must recognize that you are simply being a "copy" of other people's expectations, not your original self. You may have developed an entire personality and life that has little to do with your true self and is based on other people's left-over ideas. This is like being the biblical house built on sand. It must surely fall when it is stressed, one way or another. Certainly, this "copy" will never feel a sense of peace or fulfillment even if it manages to get by and even if it has all the material comforts of life.

Unfortunately, the pressure to be something you are not doesn't necessarily stop when you are an adult. In later life, our best friends, colleagues, and family members may try to influence our decisions and may not give us the best advice. That can happen for any number of reasons. Let's say you want to change your career or move to another city to get training for a period of time. When you talk to your best friend about this, she may try to influence your decision and persuade you not to do that. Perhaps she is jealous or she thinks that if you change your career, she won't get to spend as much time with you as she would like, or maybe she simply doesn't appreciate your real potential.

Unlimited Thinking

Regardless of what has come before in your life, you can begin to know your true self right now. You can make the decision to begin replacing the false concepts about yourself with the knowledge of your true being. You can stop being a receiver only and start creating what you want to be.

Your Silent Master is your original self still waiting to be born, to fully express itself through you. How does your Silent Master express itself? How does it create? As you have learned, it does so with thoughts and ideas. You, expressing your Silent Master, will learn to create what you desire by thinking in a new way, by thinking its thoughts. Then these thoughts and ideas will take form as your body and emotions, as events and the conditions of your life.

As soon as you contact and identify with the Silent Master within, you will begin to look at yourself and understand yourself in a new way. First and foremost, your real self thinks in unlimited ways:

What you think to be your "self" may say, "I'm such a loser." But your Silent Master says, *"I am one of a kind and I have all the power I need to develop and express my unique talents."*

Your limited self may say, "I am afraid." Your Silent Master says, *"I have no fear because I am the source of all real power and I have the strength to face and overcome any challenge."*

Your limited self may say, "Everyone tells me that my idea is crazy and there is no way I can even think about achieving this goal. I'm just wasting my time." Your Silent Master says, *"I will achieve this goal and persist until I demonstrate my truth."*

This is why you're here and why you're living now: to learn, to overcome, to grow into the fullness of your being, to find your power and your purpose and to live it. The decision to seek your Silent Master means you're in school again. Your life is your classroom. You can use all the obstacles, negatives, and limitations in your life as opportunities to demonstrate your dominion. You and your Silent Master can work together, listen to each other, and grow until you realize you are one. I call this the way of the Jung SuWon warrior.

Getting to Know All of Yourself

As you begin this journey and continue to contemplate the question "Who am I?" there are two helpful concepts to keep in mind. The first is that getting to know your true self means getting to know *all* of yourself—the physical, mental, emotional, and spiritual parts of you. If someone were to ask you what your home was like, would you only describe your living room? No, you would talk about everything—the living room, the bedrooms, the family room, the kitchen, the bathrooms, the basement. Each room has its own function and is part of your home.

Likewise, your body, mind, emotions, and spirit each have a function. They work together to create the whole package that is you. You can't unlock your full power without working with all the parts of yourself. Jung SuWon is "the way of uniting body, mind, and spirit in total harmony," and I teach my students to value, cultivate, and balance all the parts of themselves.

It always amazes me how little most of us really know about ourselves and how much we take for granted. Let's take our body, for instance. I find that when I ask people, "How well do you know yourself?" they will often say, "Well, of course I know myself. After all, I've been living with myself for all these years!" Yet when I ask them some basic questions, such as "How many bones do you have in your body, how many muscles are there in your face, or how many miles of blood vessels are in your body?" I usually get blank stares. Most people are surprised to hear that there are, in fact, 206 bones in their body and 43 muscles in their face. They are shocked to learn that if their veins, arteries, and the other vessels of their circulatory system were laid out in a line, that line would be about 100,000 miles long. That's four times around the earth. "Wow," they say, "I don't really know that much about myself."

You use your hands every day all day long—to eat, to get dressed, to lift, to write. Yet how often do you stop to think about how incredible your hand is and all the wonderful things it does for you? I'm not saying you have to become a doctor or an expert in human anatomy, but it's important to have a sense of wonder and appreciation for the body we depend upon so much. Our body is a part of who we are. If it's not functioning optimally, the other parts of us can't work at their best either. On the path to greater inner power, it's good to have a healthy curiosity and concern for how the components that make up our whole being work together.

That has a practical impact on our lives as we contemplate, for example, "If I eat this kind of food or drink this, what effect will that have on my body, my mind, my emotions?" "Why are my hands suddenly getting cramps?" "Why is my stomach hurting right now? Was it something I ate today? Is it because of my state of mind—is stress causing this?" Questions like those are part of getting to know yourself.

Your body, your mind, your emotions, your spirit—you depend on each one of these components of yourself. You can think of them as essential parts of your "team" that are meant to work together in harmony as you fulfill the purpose of your life. Doesn't it make sense, then, to truly value each one, assess whether it is performing optimally, and determine what you need to do to bring all the parts of your team into balance? You'll be learning more about the role of each of these aspects of yourself and how to call your whole team into balanced action to create the focus and power to achieve your goals.

Flow Like Water

The second concept that is helpful to keep in mind as you get to know your real self and uncover more of your inner power is this: Always leave the door open to change. Don't limit yourself or settle into a comfortable niche. Your desires, your tastes, your goals, your direction—all that may change, but your original essence will remain the same. In other words, as you explore who you are and where you want to go in your life, remember that every day is new.

What you don't like today, you may end up loving six months from now or in five years or in twenty years. If you always define yourself by your current likes and dislikes and character traits, you don't leave the door open to discovering something new and beautiful about life and about yourself that may not have been ready to emerge six months ago or five years ago or twenty years ago.

Instead, be flexible and flow like water. Water is always water. Its essence is the same, but it takes the shape of the container you pour it into. If you pour water into a round soup bowl, it takes a round shape. If you pour it into a tall, narrow vase, it is the same water but it changes shape again. We are like that water, and our surrounding environment is like the container. We may have to adapt to changing surroundings or circumstances, but the essence of our original self remains the same. That means that we need to give ourselves room to breathe, to grow, to explore, and to allow new expressions of our true self to emerge. We can't do that if we take a stubborn, self-critical, or self-limiting attitude and say, "I'm never going to do that because that's just not who I am."

When you were much younger, you may have said that you didn't like a particular type of food or person or color or music, only to find that now you love to eat that type of food, wear that color, be with that person, and listen to that type of music. For most of my life, I didn't like tasting or eating anything tart. No lemons or lemonade for me. Now I love eating lemons and I love drinking strong, tart lemonade. Our tastes can change, and that is good. It shows we are growing and evolving. So as you go through this book and learn more about yourself, don't lock yourself into a mold because you've always done things a certain way or because others you know have always done things a certain way.

Here's a story that shows how easily that can happen. Every year, a family performed a particular tradition that had been passed down the generations. The oldest male in the family would conduct the ceremony once a year each summer. Every year he would tell his son, "Pay careful attention, my boy. After I'm gone, you are going to have to carry on this tradition at your own home." The father would then walk up the steps to his porch, tie his dog to the beam in the corner, and then go about arranging the table he had set up on the porch, placing a certain kind of food and fruit and water in a specific spot on the table. When everything was set, he would ask the rest of his family to join him. He would repeat the words and rituals his own father had taught him and thank the family's ancestors for blessing them all. Dutifully his son observed every detail, committing it all to memory.

After decades, the father finally passes on and his son, now an adult, has to carry on the tradition in his own home. On the afternoon that the ceremony is to take place, he walks out to his porch and places the food, the fruit, and the water on the table all in their proper places, exactly as his father had done. Shortly before his extended family members are to arrive for the yearly ceremony, he suddenly realizes that something is missing. He doesn't have a dog to tie up in the corner of the porch because his father's dog died shortly after his father passed away. Without telling anyone, the son runs down the steps and into the village to borrow a dog that is exactly like the one his father had. He runs from house to house searching, but not a single family in his village owns a dog like the one his father had.

So he hurries down the road to the next village, but no one there has a dog like that either. He races from village to village without any luck. Now it is very dark outside and very late. Frustrated, weary, and coated with dust, he knows he must return home to tell his guests that he has failed them. The first person he sees as he slowly climbs the steps to his porch is his mother, who is sitting quietly on a chair waiting for him. She runs to him with an expression of both dismay and relief on her face. With head hanging down, he explains, "I am so sorry, Mother, but I cannot perform this ritual because I do not have a dog like father had to tie to the corner of the porch. I've been searching all this time."

"What are you talking about, my son?" she asks, her eyes wide with surprise. "Your father tied the dog to the beam in the corner of the porch so that his old friend would not disturb us during the ceremony. The dog was never a part of the ritual!"

How many times do we carry out exactly the same kind of rote performance in our own lives, just because we've always seen something done a certain way before? The son learned an important lesson that day as he came to realize that the essence and purpose of the family's ceremony—to express gratitude and ask for blessings—was what truly mattered, not every little detail of the ritual he had memorized. On the path to inner power, we can remain true to our original self *and* be flexible and flow like water as we adapt to changing conditions or obstacles.

The Real You Waiting to Be Unleashed

Moving from a limited sense of self to tapping into the power of your unlimited self does requires a change, and change can be frightening. If you want to live up to your full power and potential, however, you will have to change. When we've been sleeping in the dark, our eyes are used to the darkness. So when someone suddenly draws back the curtain and the daylight comes flooding in, don't we pull the covers over our head and moan, "Close that curtain! You're hurting my eyes!" The bright light causes discomfort at first, even pain, but that feeling eventually goes away. In the same way, your limited self may be accustomed to living in comfortable darkness. If you are willing to experience the initial discomfort that the light brings, you will soon grow accustomed to the brightness and see a whole new world illumined by the light.

As you open to a new way of seeing and being, new opportunities will come. Yes, challenges will come your way too—challenges within and without. That is part of life's journey. Yet, as we learn in the martial arts and as you'll see examples of in this book, you can use a force coming your way to your benefit. You can learn to ride the wave of those challenges to create greater growth, mastery, and overcoming. In fact, it is in facing those challenges that you will learn the most about yourself.

The way of the warrior on the path to inner power is to realize who you are in truth and to demonstrate it, a process of evolution that continues throughout your life. The work of the warrior is joyous and every encounter is an adventure. As a warrior, you know that the obstacles and limitations you confront are destined to fall because they were never a part of your real self.

No matter what challenges arise, you are never alone. Your inner strength is waiting for you right now. Your courage and creativity are waiting for you. Your excitement and dedication and discipline are waiting for you. All these qualities and more are part of your support team, waiting to be unleashed. I know you may not be used to feeling that these qualities are a part of you, and you might have some fear about what your life will be like when you step out of your comfort zone. But I promise you that you will love the sense of freedom, peace, and purpose that comes when you meet who you really are. Are you ready to experience the real you?

1. Understanding how your earliest ideas about yourself were formed will help you learn about who you are and what you have become over the years.

• Write down five positive things that others (your parents, teachers, best friends, etc.) said about you that shaped who you believe you are.

• Write down five negative things that others said about you that shaped who you believe you are.

• List five ways that you "went along" with what others wanted you to do.

2. Is there anyone in your life today who, consciously or unconsciously, has tried to hold you back from deeply exploring the question "Who am I" and following your instincts? How did that take place?

3. The big question we were asked when we were children was "What do you want to be when you grow up?" Take a moment below to visualize your childhood dreams.

• What did you want to be when you grew up?

• How does that compare to where you are now? Did you give up on a dream or have you fulfilled one?

4. It can be self-destructive to continually compare yourself to others since you are one of a kind and you have unique talents and gifts.

- In what ways do you tend to compare yourself to others rather than remind yourself that you are one of a kind?

- How has that held you back, influenced your own definition of success, or made you unhappy?

5. Your Silent Master thinks in unlimited ways. For example, when you think, "I'm a loser," your Silent Master thinks, *"I am one of a kind and I have the mental and physical strength to express my unique talents."*

- Take a piece of paper and divide it into two columns with these headings at the top:

  What I think: *What my Silent Master thinks:*

- Under the heading *"What I think,"* list some of the limitations you often think you have or the limiting ways you describe yourself when you talk to others.

- On the right side, opposite each entry you made in the first column, answer this question: "What does my Silent Master think?"

Chapter Three

The Power of Right Thinking

You MAY NOW have an inkling of what your Silent Master—your unlimited, true self—is. You know something of how it will empower you to create and shape your life according to your original, unique self. But where do you start? How do you bring forth your Silent Master in your life every day?

In your thinking right now.

The power of the Silent Master within you is the power of right thinking. The difference between a limited you and an unlimited you begins with your attitude and state of mind. So your first step in taking charge of your life is to learn to take charge of your thinking. In Jung SuWon, we do this by practicing five principles of mental conduct. Putting these principles into practice in your life will prepare you to apply the seven steps to inner power, the keys to creative thinking.

What is so important about mental conduct? Just as we obey physical rules of conduct in society so that we can function in an optimum manner, mental rules of conduct enable our creative minds to function optimally.

In chapter one, I introduced the Silent Master image entitled "Your Thoughts Create Reality." That image tells us that everything that has taken form in our life—our body, our home, our job, our relationships—first began as an immaterial "thought form," which can be a specific visual image or simply a general attitude and feeling. When you look at everything you've manifested in your life, you're looking at a picture of the quality of your thinking and feeling.

The relationship that exists between your thinking and the world you create is a universal law of manifestation. The proof that it is a law lies in your demonstrating the law. When you begin to see how your controlled thinking creates what you set out to create, you will no longer doubt the validity of this law. In fact, even little demonstrations will inspire you to greater levels of achievement. Now let's explore the preliminary steps that will prepare you to become a consciously creative thinker.

What We Think, We Create

Everything external in life was first internal in thought, so no permanent change can come about merely by attempting to fix or rearrange external conditions. Yet that's usually what we try to do. When we see the symptoms of something wrong in our lives, we usually try to get rid of the symptoms instead of getting rid of the mental condition that's causing the symptoms. Unfortunately, we tend to look only at the surface of most situations. That's because searching for the cause of a situation requires more insight than is obvious at first glance; it takes time and effort to search below surface appearances.

For example, a friend who shares my interest in gardening had an expensive plant that was dying. The leaves were turning yellow and dropping, so she spent considerable effort giving it more light, then more shade, then more plant food, then more water, then less water, and on and on. Frustrated, she brought the plant to me. I recognized that the symptoms had nothing to do with any surface problem but were from bacteria attacking the roots. I had to pull the plant out of the soil to get at the real problem. To her amazement, when I uprooted the plant, cleaned it, and replanted it, the problem disappeared. What I proved to her was that the cause of any problem must be identified before we can treat the problem effectively.

We can see other examples of our tendency to treat symptoms rather than causes in our everyday lives. A person may divorce an unsatisfactory marriage partner, only to attract another person with the same unsatisfactory characteristics or worse. Another person may go through all sorts of special programs to lose the weight, only to find that their success is short-lived—they always gain back the pounds. In both instances, the thinking (which includes attitudes and emotions as well as thoughts) that really caused the condition was not changed; therefore, the external condition did not change.

Instead of looking for the real causes, what usually happens? We most likely hear the first person declare: "You see, another failed relationship! It's like I told you—there are no good people left in this world. I have the worst luck in relationships. Even if there is somebody good for me out there, either they won't like me or I'll never find them." We may hear the second person say: "You see! I'll never be able to lose weight permanently. I may as well accept that that's just how it's going to be."

In both examples, these people are voicing the very limitation and false information about themselves that they are meant to overcome. They are basing their statements on outward material evidence. They believe their statements are true because they don't realize that they created the evidence with their own thinking! They don't realize that their statements are actually excuses for failing to challenge their beliefs and change themselves. Yes, it takes a lot of work to challenge your beliefs, a lot of courage to ask yourself if you're making true statements about yourself or simply making excuses for being lazy or weak-minded and refusing to change yourself.

This process is all the more challenging because many of our thoughts and feelings come from accepting without question what others tell us about ourselves, which is not necessarily the truth of who we are. Being a consciously creative thinker is not just about controlling your own thoughts but correcting thinking patterns that have become a part of you because you have accepted other people's opinions about yourself. That takes deep work because those opinions have become so much a part of you that it's hard to recognize them and how they have influenced you.

Teresa was forced to do the work of challenging the intense influences of others on her when the bottom began to fall out of her world. When she first came to see me, she was weak and fragile. She was having problems eating and keeping her food down, and she was extremely thin. I literally spoon-fed her in the first days I saw her, as a mother would feed a child. When I asked her how long she had been like this, she began to unfold her story.

Teresa had grown up with a father who constantly put her down. She married a man who eventually treated her worse than her father had. Her husband kept telling her that she was ugly and stupid and that it was all her fault that he had to turn to other women to fulfill his needs. None of that was true. She was not ugly and she was not stupid, as evidenced by the fact that she had a very good job with a lot of responsibility at a large corporation. Her husband's constant emotional abuse and bad behavior, including bringing other women into their house to have sex with him while Teresa was at home, was traumatic, to say the least. She started to believe all the untrue ideas he was projecting onto her, leaving her feeling utterly hopeless and ruining her self-image and self-esteem.

Even though Teresa had been seeing a psychiatrist, she still could not release the grip these thoughts had on her mind and her heart. It became so bad that she developed agoraphobia, the fear of being in crowds, public places, or open areas, and she could no longer even drive a car. Finally, someone suggested she come see me for a different approach. I asked her, as I ask all those who come to see me for the first time, "What do you want to achieve?" She told me that she really wanted to drive herself to visit her sister, who lived eight hours away in another state.

"Okay," I said, "we're going to make that happen." We had a goal and now we had to focus on getting Teresa to change the way she was thinking about herself and her capabilities. I knew she could achieve her goal, but she didn't yet believe in herself. For six months, we worked together preparing for this trip. We worked on building up her self-esteem by slowly removing all the rubbish her husband had programmed into her.

Teresa first had to understand that her husband was calling her names and feeding her lies about who she truly was in order to justify his betrayal of her. "What he is doing and saying has nothing at all to do with you," I affirmed again and again. Nevertheless, her husband's constant emotional torture—and that's what it was—had stripped her of her confidence and depleted her energy. Now she had to build up her inner and outer strength. Along with seeing me for counseling, she also began to train in martial arts. That introduced her to a power she never knew she had.

Step by step, Teresa practiced the principles of mental conduct you'll be learning here. Eventually she said she was ready to make the trip. It required tremendous courage, and I asked her to check in with me at regular intervals all along the way to her sister's home. It wasn't easy for her, but she accomplished her goal. I was very proud of her—and, more importantly, she was proud of herself. That victory was the beginning of Teresa reclaiming her life.

Think about yourself now. Are you suffering under someone

else's barrage of false ideas or toxic energy? As you review the five principles of mental conduct, which will lay the groundwork for your unlimited creative thinking, start to consider how you can use them to cleanse your mind of sabotaging ideas and connect with the magnificent power of overcoming that is inside of you. When you put these principles into practice, you will begin to eliminate the clouds of counterproductive thinking that obstruct your vision, paving the way for you to consciously create a new and fulfilling life.

THE FIVE PRINCIPLES OF MENTAL CONDUCT

Identify your fears and weaknesses and conquer them

Don't Be Afraid of Your Weaknesses

With any skill we seek to master in life, it's key to identify our areas of weakness so we can work to strengthen them. In martial arts, for example, if you don't keep your hands up in a ready position when sparring, you won't be able to effectively block a punch coming your way. You have to learn the proper form to be effective. Not all weaknesses, however, are physical. Martial arts students may know how to execute the correct form and have great physical skill, but they don't believe that by focusing their mental power and energy that their hand can break through a board or a block of cement. Their limiting belief is what's blocking their success. Likewise, overconfidence in a certain aspect of training can be a weakness, giving them an unrealistic assessment of their true skill level and of what they actually need to work on in order to improve.

In effect, when martial arts students train to break boards or cement blocks, the training is not so much about how to break through a physical object as it is about believing that they have the power within them to do that. Breaking the board is a metaphor for summoning the energy to conquer some obstacle in their lives, which they have to identify. It can be an obstacle in their relationships, their job, or some other area of their lives. So through every stage of their training, I say, "Picture the inner weakness that is holding you down and paralyzing you. Picture yourself bringing forth all your power to break through what is paralyzing you. *That's* what you are punching through and kicking out of your life."

In order to grow in mastery or attain any goal, we must know exactly what our weaknesses are. We have to be honest about what is holding us back so we can strengthen that aspect of our life. If you believe that you really deserve a promotion at work but feel your manager is ignoring you, you have to face the fact that the core of the problem may not be your performance. Instead, it may be your lack of confidence to speak up for yourself. You must believe in yourself before others can believe in you. If you are hesitant and lack confidence, others will detect that and respond to it. So, in this case, you must be willing to admit that your lack of confidence and lack of belief in yourself is a weakness. Then you must summon the courage to confidently and respectfully approach your manager and tell her that you have been doing a great job and believe you are ready for a promotion, providing the evidence to back that up.

It's difficult for most of us to identify our weaknesses, however, because we are always trying to emphasize our strengths and hide our weaknesses. If you look around at your associates, it's unlikely you'll find a person who says, "Yeah, at times I'm a mean and terrible person, but I like myself that way." More likely what you'll find are people who, in spite of their faults, defend their self-image of being a good person, of being "right," and of deserving some respect. That's to be expected because we all are a mixture of strengths and weaknesses. Most of us have an innate desire to be "good" people, and we don't like to admit that we have any faults.

One reason we don't like to admit to our faults is that most of us live life as though we're "onstage," performing roles like mother, father, breadwinner, employee, employer, student, and so on. As we perform, others constantly evaluate the strengths and weaknesses of our performances and we evaluate ourselves too. We have certain qualities, or "strengths," that tend to lead us into greater harmony and peace, and we have other qualities, or "weaknesses," that tend to undermine or sabotage the good we try to do and the full expression of our innate power.

Because we are performance oriented, we have a natural tendency to emphasize our strengths and gloss over our weaknesses. That is why social media is so popular. People want to be the star of their own movie and display their wonderful abilities and accomplishments, whether it's showing how well they can play an instrument, discipline their children, train their dogs, or critique the latest political crisis.

We all naturally like to put our best face forward. We think that gives us higher "performance ratings," and we generally believe that higher ratings in one area of life means we'll have a better life overall. But is that really true? Do we gain anything by assessing only one part of ourselves? To really put your best face forward, you must be willing to look as hard at your weaknesses as you look at your strengths and say, "I am a mixture of both." Why? So you can eliminate the weaknesses. How? By looking carefully at yourself and getting to know *all* of yourself.

When you identify and confront your weaknesses, the truth is that you have just gained an increment of power because you are taking the first step to rise above that weakness. You can't take that step when you won't admit that you even have a weakness. Life, in fact, is designed to challenge us by bringing up those weaknesses so that we can look them in the eye and choose to confront and overcome them.

Examine the Source of Your Fear

I believe that our strengths and our weaknesses are equally important to us. Both are part of the complete package that is you. There is no shame in having a weakness. All living things have their weaknesses and their strengths. It's also important to realize that what we sometimes perceive as a weakness is really a fear to try something because others have convinced us that we are not good at it.

Here is an example. Perhaps you can relate to this in an area of your own life. I met Scott when he was in his twenties when he came to me for martial arts training. For many years Scott had believed that one of his "weaknesses" was that he was a terrible singer. As part of the training I give my students, I encourage them to examine where their limiting ideas have come from and whether those ideas are really based on true facts. Oftentimes, these beliefs are based solely on the opinions others have fed them.

So Scott asked himself where the idea that he was a bad singer originally came from. It turned out that when he was in the fifth grade, Scott and his classmates were singing the song "Mr. Moon" with gusto when suddenly his teacher looked up at him and said, "Scott, your voice is terrible. Sit down and shut up."

"I tell you, that hurt—it hurt a lot," he told me. "I sat down and pretended it didn't hurt, but it did." He stopped singing then and there. He simply shut down whenever the opportunity to sing presented itself. "I might have enjoyed singing and had the potential to become a good singer," Scott admitted, "but that scene was frozen in my mind from then on."

I worked with Scott for some time to help him overcome this false belief. So certain was he that he was a terrible singer that I had to teach him to sing Korean songs because familiar English songs brought back bad memories from fifth grade and he would freeze. He needed to build up his confidence by using different sounds and ways of expression than he was familiar with.

After we worked together, Scott discovered that he liked singing and was, in actuality, a good singer. And that's the irony of this story—Scott has a beautifully deep and resonant voice. In fact, one evening at an event he attended he met a famous opera teacher from Italy, who after having a conversation with Scott told him that he had the characteristic voice of an opera singer.

I thought for a long time that one of my weaknesses was that I wasn't able to swim. I almost drowned on a couple of occasions when I was young, and ever since then I was afraid of swimming. Not long ago, I decided to challenge the belief that I couldn't swim, and I came to see that I could actually swim quite well. How did I find that out? I gave myself the chance to face that fear with the help of friends who believed in me. They were convinced that they could teach me how to swim—and their belief in me convinced me that I could do it. If others believe in you—friends, coaches, mentors—their belief, encouragement, and support can literally energize you. We can "borrow," so to speak, another's strength and expertise to help push us to the next level of mastery.

Whether we realize it or not, we do have great influence on the lives of others. Something we say or do can give others a boost or it can clip their wings. We have to make sure we don't undermine or sabotage others—and make sure we are not allowing anyone to do that to us. In other words, in whatever circumstance you are in, it's crucial to surround yourself with those who are excited about encouraging you and cheering you on to your victory. In Jung SuWon, for example, when a student is completing a level of testing but is unable at first to break a board, the teachers and other students don't whisper behind their backs, "He's no good at all. He should just give up right now." Instead, everybody cheers that person on, shouting, "You can do it! *He can do, she can do, why not me!*"

Be Objective, Not Critical

When assessing your strengths and weaknesses, be careful to be objective and not critical. If you were given a bag filled with both real and synthetic diamonds and were told to separate out the real ones, your first task would be to gain complete knowledge of the qualities of the real diamonds as well as the characteristics of the synthetic ones. As you went about the task of separating the real ones from the synthetic ones, you wouldn't impose emotional value judgments on either kind of diamond. You wouldn't say, "This wonderful, beautiful, real diamond goes in this pile," and "This disgusting, terrible, phony, synthetic one goes in that pile." No, it would be an objective, clinical undertaking designed only to create a group of real diamonds.

Here's another example. When a surgeon operates on a patient, he cannot be afraid of the amount of blood the procedure will produce or hesitate to use his knife and cut through tissue. His objective is to reach the malignancy or make the adjustment that will help his patient become well again. Let's take this hypothetical example one step further. Imagine that you are in a situation where you are not only the surgeon but also the patient. Of course that is scary. Yet you must have the courage to "operate" on yourself with the same objectivity you would use with your patients if you wish to rid yourself of what may be life-threatening.

Now apply this analogy to your own life. I'm not talking about performing real surgery on your body but looking clinically at your strengths and weaknesses and deciding where you must perform "surgery" on your character or your habits. Maybe what is really holding you back and needs to be surgically removed is the habit of drinking too much alcohol or eating too many sweets or constantly criticizing yourself or others. Remember that you don't need to make value judgments about yourself when identifying your fears, weaknesses, or strengths. When you discover that you have certain strengths, determine to keep them, but do not become overly confident or egotistical. When you find your weaknesses, determine to eliminate them, but do not fall into a mire of depression, dejection, or self-condemnation. All of us have weaknesses.

Take a moment now to reflect on your own life as if you were both doctor and patient. Relax, close your eyes, and ask yourself what sort of things in your life right now are causing you to feel unhappy, depressed, stressed, or unsuccessful? Try to identify the real cause of that unhappiness, not the symptoms alone. What mental or emotional "cancer" is holding you back that you may not have wanted to admit to yourself? For now, just think about those core weaknesses. If you want to create real happiness and fulfillment in your life, you will have to perform surgery on the cause of that emotional or mental "cancer" that is eating away at you, and you will most likely experience pain in the process. But without that, you won't be able to heal and move forward.

How will you know when you have eliminated your weaknesses? When you are no longer dominated by them. I have counseled many recovering alcoholics, and some of them were afraid to even look at a bottle. If a former alcoholic refuses to drink but is afraid to look at a bottle of alcohol, to some extent she is still being held by the disease. When she can look at the bottle and say, "I am cured, and I am not afraid of you," she is no longer dominated by the disease. In the same way, when you no longer fear that you'll fall prey to your weaknesses, you will know that you have conquered them.

The process of taking a hard look at yourself requires great energy. Maybe you don't think you're up to it or maybe you use the excuse that you'll get to it later. Yet how much energy do you think you've been expending trying to keep your weaknesses hidden? I promise that you'll be amazed at the surge of energy and relaxation you will feel when you begin to release your weaknesses.

I once watched a bird that had found a large piece of bread, much larger than what it alone could possibly eat. All the neighboring birds saw the bread and flew down from the trees to partake. The bird expended considerable energy to keep the bread away from the other birds. It was so busy taking evasive action that it didn't have time to eat the bread. To me it was obvious that if the bird would have let go of its "selfishness," there would have been enough bread for them all. The bird would have saved an enormous amount of energy by sharing.

When you are able to gain a larger view of yourself and work on intentionally releasing your most cherished weaknesses, you will experience the reward of increased energy and freedom. You needn't be afraid of your weaknesses. Your strengths alone are big enough to share with everyone and big enough to confront any situation.

Are the Weaknesses You React to in Others in You?

During the process of self-analysis, you may notice that others have weaknesses you don't have. A word of warning: Perhaps another person does indeed have some weaknesses you don't have. If, however, you find yourself reacting, especially reacting emotionally to a person's weakness, there is a 99.9 percent chance that you also have that weakness within you.

For instance, you may find yourself saying, "I hate the way

Julie acts with such little confidence in herself. It seems like she's afraid of her own shadow! I don't even like to be around her because her fear bothers me so much." There is a good possibility that the reason you don't want to be around Julie is because she's acting out *your* fear and *your* lack of confidence. You may be so afraid of this weakness in yourself that you refuse to see it in yourself. So when you see it in Julie (which you think is safer to do), you react only to Julie when you should be observing it and facing it in yourself as well.

It's a fact, then, that sometimes our weaknesses are hard to see and to remove merely because we are afraid of them. But think of it this way. When you have an ugly wart or growth on your skin, you have no desire to keep it. Even if you hide it from sight, you keep thinking of how you will get rid of it. Regard your weaknesses the same way. They are not necessarily as visible as warts are, but they are just as "unsightly" and can detract from your mental ease and beauty to the same extent.

Anger, fear, resentment, laziness, despair, pessimism, selfishness, arrogance, revenge, sarcasm, criticism, jealousy, worry—these are only a few of the weak, powerless states of mind to be conquered. You'll know you're well on your way to conquering these characteristics when you find yourself reacting with compassion to them in another or in yourself. Compassion is one of the qualities of your Silent Master and signals the presence of your Silent Master beginning to operate in your mind. Compassion also means that you have lost your fear of the weakness, and that is the first step to removing it.

The second step to removing your weakness is to replace it with a quality that negates it, one that is the opposite of the bad quality. You'll learn more about that process later. What's important now is to understand that weaknesses are not part of your original self. By replacing your weaknesses with strengths—replacing anger with love, laziness with action, selfishness with selflessness, and so on—you will have done everything you need to do to conquer these enemies of your well-being.

Be aware, too, that there is a flip side to the tendency to see our own weaknesses in others: sometimes we don't see our own beauty and innately good qualities, even though we recognize them in others. When I see people admiring someone who is accomplished or when they say to me, "Wow, even though you've gone through all those hardships, you've been able to do such wonderful things with your life," I know in my heart that they are seeing a reflection of some part of themselves. I usually respond, "Thank you very much. I want you to know that from my point of view, you didn't just describe me (or such and such a person); you described who *you* are." That is true because we can only truly recognize the greatness in others if we have within ourselves that same quality. We see ourselves through other people. They are a mirror, helping us recognize both our weaknesses and our strengths.

Learn from your mistakes

Mistakes Are Your Feedback System

The second principle of mental conduct is to learn from your mistakes. In the preceding section, I talked about how we are constantly evaluating ourselves as if we are onstage and how we tend to hide our weaknesses to put ourselves in a better light, thereby hoping to give ourselves a higher performance rating. For the same reason, we tend to hide our mistakes. Just as we think a good performer shouldn't be weak, we think a good performer shouldn't make mistakes. So when we do make a mistake, we believe that the more quickly we can get it out of sight and move on, the better. Think about that for a moment. When we have made a mistake, one of the things we immediately do is try to cover it up, make excuses for it, or justify it. We'll do almost anything to get away from it rather than look long and hard at it.

What we don't realize is that mistakes are part of a natural feedback system when we are learning a task or accomplishing a goal. That's all.

Imagine a gymnastics student learning to do a back flip for the first time. As he strives to imitate the movement as best he can, the teacher tells him two things: what he did correctly and what he did incorrectly. That is called positive and negative feedback. The positive feedback describes his right action and the negative feedback describes his mistakes. Can you see how knowledge of mistakes is as important in the learning process as knowledge of right actions? When you know what is not correct, you can consciously strive to avoid the mistake and duplicate the right action. Precise knowledge of what is correct and incorrect, then, forms the basis of our conscious choices and actions, and that speeds up the learning process.

Now imagine a person striving to get promoted in her workplace. Perhaps she calls attention to herself by bragging and showing off. To make herself look better, she calls attention to deficiencies in co-workers. After a while, she is fired instead of promoted. Did she make a mistake? Absolutely. She must now regard that mistake as feedback on what *not* to do to get a promotion. She still has to learn what she needs to do, of course, and may make more mistakes in the process of finding the right action to take.

The key is to keep going. She must not let her mistakes be excuses for giving up or allow her self-condemnation to paralyze her future actions. If her goal is worth achieving, she must be willing to persist through every form of failure, always regarding it as a learning experience, as feedback, until she hits upon the right action for success.

Making Mistakes Is Essential to Progress

Willingness to learn from mistakes is the backbone of all progress. How many mistakes do you think Alexander Graham Bell made in inventing the first telephone that connected one room in his house to another? Now technology allows us to see the person we're speaking with on the other side of the globe. How many mistakes did the engineers make while developing that technology? Who cares? The object is to succeed, not to count your mistakes.

Mistakes are part of the natural process of striving to make constant improvements in your life. Mistakes are essential to your progress. In fact, without mistakes, you can't be successful. The minute you decide to work toward achieving a goal that is important to you, you will make mistakes. How did we humans get the idea that to be perfect we couldn't make mistakes? Never making a mistake does not make us perfect. Never *repeating* a mistake after we learn from it is as perfect as we need to be.

In the face of a mistake, stay motivated and remind yourself that it is part of your path to success—that making mistakes is essential because it helps you to become better and better as you practice. Imagine the freedom you'll feel when you don't have to worry about defending or hiding your mistakes. Experience the increased energy that comes from this freedom! Welcome your mistakes into your consciousness as your friends and teachers.

If you do that and are determined to learn from mistakes, you will also gain a precious gift: *wisdom.* There is a big difference between knowledge and wisdom. Knowledge is something you gain by looking up information on the internet, in an encyclopedia, or in books or other resources. Wisdom, however, comes from experience. You don't gain wisdom by reading or absorbing information; you only gain it through experience. When I interview applicants for a job at one of my businesses, I always look at how much real-world experience they have and what hardships and challenges they have had to face and overcome. I find that those who are willing to learn from mistakes and take on new challenges develop a resiliency and inner strength that gives them the edge on the job and in their personal lives.

Fear of Making Mistakes Is Mental Laziness

Part of our fear of mistakes is pure laziness. What's the worst thing that will happen if you make a mistake? You will have to abandon that course of action and take another, which means, in short, a lot of work. It means you will have to think of another course of action. You may have to be creative. You may have to expend energy in thinking, evaluating, planning. You may have to resist emotions such as despair, futility, rejection, and fear.

If you are mentally lazy, making mistakes will be one of the best excuses you have for giving up, for deciding that maybe your goal isn't so important after all. What a senseless waste that would be. Why expect so little out of life and out of yourself?

Mistakes are not harmful in and of themselves. What is harmful is our attitude toward mistakes. If you are willing to make mistakes, look at them, regard them as feedback, and keep right on making them until you achieve your goal, you have the right attitude. You won't purposely make mistakes, of course. But because you are challenging yourself, you will be aware that mistakes are a natural part of the process. Having the right attitude toward mistakes, the right view of them, will give you the freedom to pursue your goals with confidence, with minimum distraction, and with your success securely focused in your mind. When you find yourself joyfully moving from one situation to another, using mistakes for learning, growing, and improving, you will know that your Silent Master is beginning to operate in your life.

Know that you have the ability to do, the capacity to act, and the capability to perform and produce

---

Taking Command of the Creative Process

Consider again the second Silent Master image you learned about in the previous chapter: "Your Silent Master consciousness was born out of the infinite life force creating and animating the universe. . . . Because you are this consciousness, whatever qualities the life force possesses, you possess also." You and the universe are inseparable. You are a unit; you are one. Since the life force of the universe is creative, you are creative also. It is the nature of our universe that thought takes form. Therefore, because you are an integral part of our universe, your thinking takes form.

You have been creating your life since the day you were born. As the fourth Silent Master image tells us: "Your Silent Master knows itself as the source of mental, emotional, and material energy—*your* energy, which you are free to utilize and control in creating what you desire. Therefore, you are a co-creator, cooperating with the life force of the universe to shape yourself and the world around you."

The life force of the universe flows through you and beats your heart. When you think, you use its energy to create other forms of energy, and this energy literally materializes, or takes form as matter. So everything material, both objects and events, is a "crystallization" of thought energy. The artist and musician illustrate this process quite naturally in their work. Don't they take an intangible thought or feeling and turn it into something tangible—a painting or a symphony?

You have already been creating your life. That process is the gift to you from the life force of the universe. Unless you have trained your mind to do otherwise, however, your creative process has been largely unconscious and therefore undirected, somewhat haphazard, influenced by other people's thinking, and limited by your restricted awareness of what you think is possible. The purpose of the third principle of mental conduct is to emphasize how you limit yourself *by yourself.* You limit your thinking *with your thinking.* This principle tells you to wake up, open up, expand your expectations, and realize that you can achieve and produce whatever you can think if you back it up with the right actions.

What is it you really want? This is not an invitation to be frivolous in your thinking. If anything, this is a warning to be extremely careful about what you think. Why? Because all thought truly does take form one way or another. There is some truth in the expression "Be careful what you wish for; you just might get it."

Let me exaggerate to make this point clear. What if you have a desire to see blue snowflakes falling on pink- and yellow-striped rocks in the middle of a desert? Do you realize that such a scene is possible to create with today's design technology and software? Even that thought has a way to take form. Our modern-day technology has developed progressively to reveal greater capabilities for unlimited expression and communication of thought.

It's really very simple how the law of creation works. Negative energy creates negative manifestations. Hateful thoughts create broken relationships, wars and weapons, physical diseases of all kinds. Positive energy creates positive manifestations. Loving thoughts create harmonious organizations, cooperative govern-ments, and the healing of all kinds of discord.

While the law of manifestation may be easy to understand, it's more difficult to identify and remove the ways of thinking that produce destructive manifestations. Yet isn't that why we're here—to learn to take charge of what we manifest by taking charge of our thinking? Can you see now that you can be your own worst enemy because you're the one who monitors what you think? Who thinks your thoughts? Others can suggest thoughts to you, but you're the one who accepts or rejects what to entertain in your mind.

In this process of learning to take charge of your thinking, remember not to criticize yourself. Instead, be your own best friend. When you find yourself uncomfortable with your own neg-ative creations and wanting to change your thinking, in actuality you are feeling the presence of your Silent Master. Your discomfort signals that you know something better is possible. Your Silent Master always urges you to grow into greater freedom from any sort of limitation. Previously, you may have been willing to accept being poor, being sick, having a job you dislike. Now you know you don't have to accept anything except your freedom—your gift from the universe to create whatever you desire.

Be Realistic

Of course, you'll still need to take positive action to reach your goals. You may have to enroll in school to get trained in a skill or profession. You may have innate talent to paint or draw, but you need to learn how to use the right tools and techniques to hone your skills so you can express your talent. It takes action to achieve this. You can't just wait for things to come to you. You have to invest your time and energy in the change you want to make. I've had people complain to me that they are lonely and they can't seem to make friends. When I find out how they spend their free time—sitting at home in front of the television—I ask the obvious: "How can anyone reach out to talk to you and make friends with you if you're always hiding away by yourself?"

You have to be realistic when you are working toward any goal. When you want to buy a car, don't you plan it out? You have in mind what color car you want, whether you want a two-door or four-door car, an SUV or a pickup truck. You know you can save so much money a month and therefore what kind of car you can afford. That's being realistic. The same realism and analysis applies to all your goals.

The flip side of this is that people sometimes say, "That goal is simply not realistic," when, in fact, it is within their reach with a little creative thinking. Here's an example, and one I come across often with young adults I counsel. When I spoke with a young man recently about saving money each month to put toward buying his own home in the future, he said, "I can't do that because I don't have any money to save." Colin claimed that on his current salary, after paying for his car loan, his food, rent, phone bills, and other necessities, he didn't have a cent left.

This surprised me, so I suggested we go over his expenses to see exactly where he was spending his money. When we looked at the list together, I noticed that Colin was spending more than a thousand dollars a month on food just for himself. "Okay," I said. "Help me out. What are you eating? Are you sprinkling gold in your salad dressing? Are you really spending that much on food?" What I learned was that he was eating out at restaurants for breakfast, lunch, and dinner. He had no idea he was spending anywhere near that amount of money on food.

I explained to Colin that eating out for every single meal wasn't necessary and it wasn't healthy either. If he didn't break this habit now, someday when he was married he and his wife would find themselves spending two thousand dollars a month on food. I also told him that the core issue wasn't how much money he was making at his job right now but how well he was managing that money. Even if he earned one hundred thousand dollars a month but spent it here and there without thinking realistically about his budget, he would have no money left to save.

So I suggested that for one month Colin try not eating out and instead learn about the food he could buy and how to cook healthy meals. As an added plus, I told him, your future wife will be very happy that you know how to shop and cook. "Say to yourself, 'I only have so much to spend on my food,' and see how you can manage to do that," I encouraged him. "This will teach you to manage your meal bills and it will also teach you to practice awareness and visualization. While you are shopping at the grocery store, you'll have to visualize what you want to cook for yourself." I suggested he take on the goal of trying to cut the amount of money he was spending on food in half. If he could do that, he would be able to put the other five hundred dollars in the bank each month.

Colin didn't think that was possible at first, but he committed to giving it a try. He went shopping each week and started to learn how to cook healthy meals. It took him a few months to get into the rhythm of doing this, but he stuck with it and amazed himself. Colin is now saving five hundred dollars every single month. In addition, he is in better shape because he is eating healthier food, he's appreciating his food, and he is excited to be learning how to cook.

Be Practical and Confident

The third principle of mental conduct—know that you have the ability to do, the capacity to act, and the capability to perform and produce—tells you that the possibilities are endless when you tap into your inner power and are proactive and persistent. Anyone who has achieved a goal they have long held in mind will tell you that it required consistency, mental discipline, and dedication on their part. With some prodding and encouragement, another young man I coached proved that for himself and increased his confidence and self-esteem in the process.

Adrian was working in a low-paying factory job. He was bored and unhappy. When I asked him what he really wanted to do for a living, he said, "I'd really like to work with computers."

"Okay," I said, "so what's stopping you?"

"Well," he replied, "I don't know how to do it. I don't have the education to work with computers."

Many times when I ask people what they would really like to do, they name something but then immediately follow it with a reason why they think they cannot do it. That reason is usually based on nothing more than a limited belief.

I helped him see that aiming for this goal was not rocket science. All he needed to do was get some training in his chosen field. I told Adrian, as I tell all the people I coach, that it doesn't matter how old you are. Education is not limited to those of a certain age. Knowledge is not limited by age. Knowledge belongs to anybody who really wants it.

Some people hide behind excuses like "I'm too old to do that now," but that's a cop-out. "Why are you letting excuses dominate your life?" I ask them. "*This moment* is your time. Your Silent Master is telling you to get moving now. And it's better to get engaged and work toward your goal now before you get even older and it gets harder!"

I helped Adrian to find out where to get the foundational training he needed. After he had gone through a few months of training, I asked him to write down where he wanted to work. He shook his head and said, "I don't know how to do this." Now, I didn't ask him *how* he was going to work at the place he wanted to work. I only asked him *where* he would like to work. There's a difference. After thinking about it, he told me he would like to work at a certain type of IT company doing a certain kind of job. I next instructed him to learn how to write a resume and send it out to those kinds of companies.

He did, and to his surprise he was soon offered an entry-level job at one of those companies. But he told me that he was not sure he should accept the job because it paid ten cents an hour less than his wages at the factory where he was currently working. I couldn't believe that he would even consider going back to his job in the factory and give up on his dream because of ten cents. I explained to him that this new job wasn't going to be his last job and that he should use his time there to learn about how the corporate world works, how to be a team player as well as how to stand his ground, how to manage timelines and relationships, and how to communicate with others effectively.

"You'll have the opportunity to interact with a team of people and get an invaluable education," I told him. "That is better than attending Stanford University! You're going to learn what's happening in the real world. Are you going to tell me that for ten cents an hour you're going to give that up?"

Then came more excuses. "I think they've already hired somebody," he said.

"Go to their offices right away," I told him. "Don't wait. Knock on their door and show them that you really want that job before the opportunity is gone." That's exactly what he did, and in the end he got the job. After six months, I asked him if he felt more confident than he had six months ago, and he said he did. He had grown a lot during his short time at this job, both personally and in his technical skills.

Now it was time for the next step. I recommended that he update his resume once again and apply for a new and better position. This time, it didn't matter to him how much he was going to get paid because he understood the value of the experience he would gain. He got a position in a new company, and after six months I encouraged him to update his resume once again and apply for a new job. His long-term goal had been to work at Xerox, and in a relatively short period of time he was offered a job there.

In a matter of a few years and lots of hard work, Adrian qualified himself to get better and better positions, and in the process he quadrupled his salary. More importantly, he gained self-confidence and self-esteem. Just think—he almost didn't allow himself to experience that transformation in his life because he was initially concerned about making ten cents less an hour. With motivation, the belief that we have within us "the ability to do, the capacity to act, and the capability to perform and produce," and down-to-earth practicality, we *can* achieve our dreams.

Have determination and a quality purpose

Be Specific

Now you know that you have the freedom to create and you know the law: *what you think, you create*. The fourth principle of mental conduct invites us to engage the power of our determination and, as importantly, to use our power responsibly in invoking this law.

When you decide to make a change, achieve a goal, or create something new in your life, first be sure to focus your objective clearly in your mind and be specific. At my seminars, I ask the attendees to write down their specific goals. Many times, what they write is too general and vague. You need to be specific, writing down and visualizing the exact details of what you want to achieve.

The thought "I desire a change in my social life" will take form somehow, but it may be so vague and indistinct that you won't notice a change. "I desire to meet more people" is better. "I desire to meet more people who share my interest in flying airplanes (or whatever)" is better still. If your goal is to become so accomplished in your profession that you receive an award, write down the name of the awards ceremony, the date and time it will take place, the location of the event, and the dress or suit you'll be wearing.

Focus as specifically as possible on what you want to accomplish. As I said earlier, when you want to buy a car, you identify the kind of car you want and the make, model, color, and accessories you desire. When you take a vacation, you plan exactly where you want to go, where you will stay, and how you will get there, and you proceed to make all the proper arrangements. You are being specific, aren't you? The even greater goals in your life deserve as much care and focus, don't they? Know the details about the goals you want to reach and the steps you'll need to take to get there. Be specific and then focus your will and unflinching determination behind your purpose.

I can't emphasize enough how important it is to identify your goals for yourself. You cannot give that power to others. You can listen to your parents, your friends, or your colleagues, but you are the only one who knows what you really desire and what you really want to accomplish. Isn't it true that when you know you are in love with someone, no one can tell you otherwise? Not even your best friend can convince you to love someone else, even though they may try. Likewise, you and only you can identify what goals you are passionate about and then take charge of achieving them.

Another key to setting your goals and being specific is to make sure you don't spread your energy too thin by giving yourself too many options. Having too many options in life confuses us, and we can't keep up with everything we are considering. If you have too many options and give yourself too many choices, you'll be continually saying, "Should I do this? Should I do that?" That uses up energy—the energy you need to direct into achieving your goals. I always say to people, imagine you are like Robinson Crusoe, alone on his desert island. When you're on an island, there's not much there and you have few choices. In the same way, narrow down your choices and then focus on those.

Be Determined

Once you articulate your goal in specific terms, be consistent in your determination to achieve it. Here's the thing about determination: it works only when you put it to work. Let's say you paid a tailor one thousand dollars in advance to produce evening clothes to wear to a special event. This event will never happen again, and the clothes are designed for this one evening. Will you go to pick up your new clothes even if it's raining heavily? Yes. Will you go if you're angry about getting a late start because the stew boiled over in your kitchen? Yes. Will you go if you find one of the streets on the way is blocked by road construction? Yes—you'll take a detour. Will you continue even if the freeway traffic is totally stopped and you have to sit for two hours? Yes. What will you do when you arrive at the tailor's shop right after he has hung up his "closed" sign? You'll bang on the door until he lets you in.

When you're looking for a new job or considering another major step in your life, do you have the same determination? Where does all this determination go after a few rejections? Where does it go when, after more failures than you expected, you feel afraid and dejected? Are your new clothes really so much more deserving of your determination than you are?

When we get discouraged, we can make all sorts of excuses. Don't allow that to be the case for you. People who don't have arms but really want to paint learn how to paint with a brush in their mouth or they use their feet. They don't let the fact that they don't have arms stop them. No matter what, they find a way. People who have no legs still run and ski, don't they? They use prosthetics. No one can stop them from doing what they love. Now think about what you may have used as an excuse not to follow through on your dreams. You may have even called it an obstacle. But is it really an obstacle—or an excuse?

Determination is born out of a hunger and passion in your life. You've got to be hungry to achieve your dreams and your goals. You can't just brag about what you want and then give up on it. That's treating your dreams and goals like a hobby. There's a big difference between a hobby and a goal. A real goal is a life-and-death matter.

What are your burning life goals? And are you so hungry to achieve them that nothing will stand in your way? I was told a million times in my life: *You cannot do that, no matter what.* I refused to accept those limitations. If I could break through centuries of cultural taboos against women being trained in the martial arts and if I arrived in the United States from a foreign country with no money and knowing no English and was able to get to where I am today, I know that you can make your dreams happen too.

Unswerving determination is one of the most important factors in reaching any goal. Only you can make your determination work for you. If you use it, your determination will attract to you the right associates, the right information, the ability to be in the right place at the right time, and all the other factors you need for your success. Determine now to value determination.

It doesn't matter what age you are or what external condition you now find yourself in. Your determination can transcend outer conditions. Take Chef Jeff Henderson, for example. At twenty-four, he was already in prison for dealing drugs and spent ten years behind bars. Normally people in a situation like this, where nothing seems to be going right and life seems hopeless, just give up. But he did not give up. He was determined to learn as much as he could and improve himself. While he was in prison, he worked his way up through the ranks of service in the kitchen and realized that he had a passion for cooking. He decided that when he was released from prison, he would become a chef.

Can you imagine the obstacles an African American man with no formal culinary training and a criminal background would face in reaching that goal? But face them he did to become not only the executive chef at several top restaurants in Las Vegas but also a *New York Times* bestselling author and an inspirational speaker with his own popular reality TV show. What got him there? He knew exactly what he wanted to achieve and he pursued that goal with unmitigated passion, perseverance, and determination. By changing what he thought about himself and what he was capable of achieving, he literally changed his reality. Instead of doing nothing, shutting down, or feeling as if he had no power, as many do when they feel literally or figuratively imprisoned, he saw opportunity. Even in the worst conditions, you can use some element of your situation to make choices that will move you forward and spur your creativity in some way.

An episode in the life of Steve Jobs reveals the same kind of determination. He is famous for a lot of things, but here's something you may not know about him. Six months after he had enrolled in college, he dropped out because he didn't want his parents to spend their life's savings paying his tuition when he really didn't know what he wanted to do with his life. He decided to stay on campus, though, sleeping on the floor of his friends' rooms and returning Coke bottles to get the five-cent deposit so he could buy food. Determined to get the most out of his time there, he audited a few classes, including a calligraphy class.

Looking back at that experience, Jobs said years later, "What I stumbled into by following my curiosity and intuition turned out to be priceless later on. . . . Ten years later, when we were designing the first Macintosh computer, it all came back to me." Inspired by what he had learned in that seemingly impractical class, Jobs created his first Mac with something no one had seen before—a choice of multiple typefaces and proportionally spaced fonts instead of the boring monospace alphabet. The average person could now choose and design using their preferred type. Though we take it for granted today, it was revolutionary then. With his energy and drive, Steve Jobs turned something he had learned years earlier into a creative breakthrough. When you are determined to succeed and you have a mindset of resiliency and resourcefulness, you use all that has come before to create the next breakthrough in your life.

In the martial arts, as I mentioned, we look to nature for inspiration and guidance when developing the qualities that express our inner power. I like to use the analogy of wild grass as a reminder of the value of determination. We don't really think of grass as something worth appreciating, except perhaps on a golf course. Wild grass, however, plays an important role. The roots work together and become so united that they provide the vital function of protecting land and soil to prevent landslides.

There's a kind of silent language in nature, if you want to put it that way, that is spoken between the land, the rivers, the grasses, everything. After a tsunami, when the flood waters eventually recede, a whole new landscape appears. What is the first thing that emerges after the waters subside? Grass—the same grass that has the power to find its way between cracks of cement and can even break through rock when it needs to. It seems like a miracle when the grass appears, but it is simply following its natural instinct, responding to the silent language and harmonizing connection between all the elements of nature. We, too, can call on that same inner resiliency and determination.

Be a Responsible Creator

The other aspect of the fourth principle of mental conduct is having a quality purpose. Because we have such great freedom to create, we must be responsible and use our power constructively.

Remember, you can have whatever you can think. This even holds true for the person plotting to rob a bank. His plan may certainly take material form and "succeed," but, just as importantly, other thoughts that are the foundation for the decision to rob the bank will also take form. Our would-be robber may be driven by thoughts such as "My parents never cared about me, society doesn't care about me, no one has ever done a single thing to help me. So why should I have to work hard? Society owes me big time. No one is ever going to look out for me, so I just need to take what I want."

All those limiting thoughts and more will ultimately take form, either as a literal prison or, if the robber is not apprehended, as a prison of poverty, despair, fear, and loneliness. This person has free will and will create exactly what he has thought. Clearly, however, this person does not have a quality purpose and is not using his power constructively.

Your true desires, those longings for certain goals that feel like a part of you, are given to you from your Silent Master. Therefore, you have every right to put your purpose, will, and determination behind them to make them manifest.

If you ever have any doubt about whether a certain desire is worthy of your total energy and attention, the key is to look at the supporting beliefs behind that desire. That will give you your answer. You may say, for instance, "I desire to build a new house." Let's consider two different sets of supporting thoughts behind this desire. First, suppose you say, "I want a new house because my brother has a better one than I have." If that's the case, be prepared to manifest some other unsavory thoughts that are necessarily part of this picture, such as "I'm not valuable in and of myself. My worth is measured by how well I stand up to someone else. I am never quite as good as someone else, so I constantly have to play catch-up. My decisions are based on what I have to do to compete, not on what I really want to do; therefore, I'm not able to make my own decisions. I'm too busy reacting instead of acting. I don't value who I am, so I feel the need to be jealous."

Do you see how far-reaching a single thought or desire can be?

On the other hand, suppose you say, "I want a new house because my family members and I need more space and privacy to pursue our individual projects without interfering with each other." Supporting thoughts that are part of that picture include such thoughts as "My family and I are pursuing worthwhile activities. We respect individual differences, and we believe we should follow the path of our choosing unobstructed. We value family harmony. There is room for individuals to fulfill their needs while also being part of a group. A growing and expanding house supports each of our abilities to grow and expand." Would you like to manifest all those thoughts as well as the new house? I think so. Do you see now the importance of identifying the supporting thoughts behind your desire? You will manifest those supporting thoughts as well as your desire.

Generally, you will know your desire is true and comes from

your Silent Master when you have a calm sense of peace as you visualize your desire in your mind. You will have a feeling not unlike love when you think about this desire. If your desire passes the test of having positive, worthwhile supporting thoughts, then throw all your energy into making it happen. You now know that you *can* make it manifest. That ability is a gift from the universe to you, a fundamental law of your being. If you find that the real supporting thoughts behind your desire are not positive and worthwhile, the tools you'll find throughout this book will help you refocus and tap into the strength and wisdom within you to achieve your true goals.

Have a positive mental attitude

Emotions Are Batteries of Creative Power

So far I've emphasized the mental activities occurring in the "thinking" part of your consciousness. In addition, there is a "feeling" part of you, the part of your consciousness that experiences emotion. Your feelings and emotions play a large role in what you manifest or fail to manifest. If you compare your thoughts to seeds, your emotional environment is the soil in which they are planted. Your positive seeds must be sown in positive soil to grow and flourish. Together, your positive thoughts and feelings create a positive mental attitude. The fifth principle of mental conduct—have a positive mental attitude—highlights how this state of mind is essential if you are going to break through to awesome in your life.

Note how we can use the word *attitude* almost interchangeably with the phrase *state of mind*. An attitude is a mental focus and consists of thoughts, beliefs, and emotions (feelings), all of which will result in some kind of behavior. Your behavior, then, reflects all the qualities of your attitude because what we call our attitude is a creative force behind our actions and creations.

The word *attitude* comes from the Latin root word *aptitudo*, which means "fitness" or "aptitude." So attitude is literally related to the concept of aptitude or capability. Your attitude has everything to do with what you are capable of achieving. Therefore, in this section we will carefully analyze how to create the positive attitude that is responsible for your success and achievement.

This Silent Master image again relates here: "Your Silent Master knows itself as the source of mental, emotional, and material energy—*your* energy, which you are free to utilize and control in creating what you desire." Emotions are batteries of power; they contribute tremendous energy in the creative process of transforming thought into form. Your emotions are your friends when they constructively accompany and support your creative thinking. They are your enemies when they sabotage and conflict with your mental objectives. Your emotions also constantly give you feedback about the quality of your thinking.

You may have heard about the power of positive thinking before, but I want to help you take this understanding beyond just a mental concept by giving you some insights into how important your emotions are and how to handle them. If you are trying to make a change in your life or achieve a goal, take a look at your emotional state, not only the feelings you have that are related to your goal. You may find that in order to succeed you may need to clean away negative feelings you are harboring, even if those feelings seem unrelated to your goal. You may be trying to create a new career and are thinking quite positively about that goal, but if your emotional condition is presently full of anger and resentment over a broken relationship, that is negative emotional soil that will not help your new thought-seeds grow.

A key point to keep in mind is that your emotions don't come out of nowhere; they follow thoughts. The positive or negative emotions you feel are a result of an idea you have first. If, for instance, you are feeling the emotion of anger, the thought creating the emotion may be something like "I am being blocked, I am being deceived, I can't get my way." A feeling of affection may be created by thoughts like "I value this person's honesty and I desire to express my appreciation."

Sometimes, however, your emotions appear to come out of nowhere, and sometimes they seem to conflict with what you're thinking. You may say, "I'm thinking as positively as I can about this situation, but I'm still depressed." What's wrong? If thought creates emotion, how is it possible to have emotions that conflict with your thinking? The answer is, you may have formed *invisible* thoughts that are now creating emotions.

Conflicts between the Mind and Emotions

To understand where invisible thoughts come from, you must realize that you have a conscious mind (accessible to your immediate awareness) and a subconscious mind (outside of your immediate awareness). The prefix *sub* means underneath; so by definition, you have thoughts and feelings "underneath" your conscious mind that you are not aware of. You are, however, affected by those thoughts and feelings. Although you are not aware of them, they still operate.

What is your subconscious mind? It is a storehouse of everything you have experienced, all your thoughts, feelings, memories—all the programming you've experienced since you were born. It is like an amazingly accurate video and audio recorder of your entire experience. It is *sub*conscious because your conscious mind was not designed to hold this volume of information. Your conscious mind has a different responsibility: it processes only the information you need to function in the present moment. To open a can of soup, you don't need to remember the color of the baby crib you slept in (which is stashed away in your subconscious).

Fortunately, your conscious mind can "ask" your subconscious mind for information, and the information can suddenly become conscious. Your conscious mind is similar to the cursor on a computer screen. It goes where you direct it. "What was the name of that blond-haired girl I liked in the second grade?" you may wonder. While you're doing the dishes two days later, you suddenly remember. Or you may wonder "Why is it that when I see Tom, I feel like painting?" You may suddenly become aware that Tom looks exactly like an old friend in your high-school art class. The cursor (your conscious mind) doesn't need to know the contents of the program or how the computer functions (your total consciousness). Its only function is to select and focus.

Sometimes, however, subconscious information is difficult to obtain precisely because you don't know everything that it contains. By definition this information is outside your conscious awareness. You may not know what information to ask for. When this happens, conflicts between your thoughts and emotions occur.

Here's an illustration. Suppose you are in a martial arts or other kind of training program and you have decided to give up drinking alcoholic beverages during this time to help you stay clear-minded and focused. You have a quality purpose and determination, and everything is going well in your training. At your workplace nothing has changed, yet you notice that whenever you have a conference with your boss, you have an irresistible desire to go home and drink until you are buzzed. Despite your best efforts and willpower, you give in to this urge each time, and you don't know why. Now you feel miserable and depressed, which affects your training.

The cause of this urge to drink could be subconscious programming. You could, for example, have a memory of your infant anxiety being quelled by drinking. Subconsciously, not consciously, you remember that every time you were anxious, uncomfortable, upset, and crying, you received a bottle of comforting liquid that helped you escape the feeling of anxiety and thus stopped your crying. In this example, the conferences with your boss are stimulating feelings of discomfort and anxiety that you are not facing in an effective manner. Hence, the old programming kicks in, and you find yourself seeking the same solution: drinking a liquid that kills pain, just as milk comforted you long ago.

The same is often true for those who cannot seem to lose weight or whose weight goes up and down like a yo-yo. Say as a baby you felt sick or lonely and you started crying. What's the first thing you mother did when she heard you crying? She gave you a bottle of milk, even though you weren't crying because you were hungry. So because of that programming, whenever you feel stressed or depressed today, you automatically search for some food to put into your mouth because that's what you've been taught to do. You think to yourself subconsciously, "I'm stressed. I'm not feeling well. I remember that my mom gave me food to comfort me. So that's what I'll do now."

You are, of course, totally unaware of this programming. Here you are, putting all your energy into giving up alcohol or losing weight, but you're being sabotaged by invisible thoughts about how to relieve pain. Because you're not aware of what's going on, you don't attack the real cause of the problem; you attack yourself instead. "I'm weak," you may affirm. "I'm such a loser." As a result, you feel dejected, hopeless, and self-critical, feelings which do not lead to a positive mental attitude. You cannot reach your goal under those circumstances. You have a conflict. Your mind is saying, "I want to give up drinking," but your emotions are saying, "I feel helpless and powerless because I can't do it."

Ask for Insight and Direction

When you are experiencing a conflict between your mind and emotions, you can turn to your Silent Master consciousness. It operates over both your conscious and subconscious mind: "Your Silent Master is completely aware, infinitely intelligent, and ready to give you all the insight, information, and direction you need to fulfill your dreams, ambitions, and goals."

You can affirm that you and your Silent Master are one. Then, by simply *knowing* you have this unlimited awareness and intelligence available to you, you can ask for information regarding your obstacle, whatever it may be. Asking is as simple as mentally posing the question to yourself and expecting the answer to come into your conscious awareness. However long or short a time it takes, the answer will surely come. You may be led to people, books, or situations that will ultimately assist you, and you *will* get your answer.

Your real self already knows its freedom from mental and emotional limitations. Therefore, you can insist on experiencing the feelings of your real self. These are always positive feelings, which you can claim as your own. In addition, you can consciously strive to entertain thoughts that bring you the most positive feelings.

There is a good reason why positive emotions such as joy, optimism, love, compassion, affection, hope, and gratitude help you achieve your goals. They bring forth the presence of your Silent Master and therefore have creative power. A positive mental attitude simply means that you are free from conflicting thoughts and emotions. You feel emotions of joy, peace, and confidence because you *expect* success. You feel strong because you realize that your real self has power, and you have removed (or are removing) all negative thoughts and emotions that could obstruct your manifestation.

Deal Wisely with Negative Emotions

You may be thinking: theoretically that's all encouraging, but right now I feel depressed or lonely or afraid or overwhelmed. What do I do right now? Here are two steps you can take immediately.

The first step is that when you feel negative, acknowledge that you feel negative. That may seem overly simplistic, but you would be surprised how often we refuse to acknowledge that we're feeling angry or depressed. When you ignore your emotions, you will always see some kind of symptom emerging as a result. If you aren't able to express your anger in a healthy way, you may develop a headache. If you are an effective emotion-dodger, you'll say that the physical symptom is due to some other cause. Be aware that you may have become quite an expert at denying emotions, which creates quite a Pandora's box of physical illnesses, misdirected reactions, covert aggression, and inexplicable emotional outbursts.

Ask yourself, too, whether you deny your good feelings as well as the negative ones. Trying to push away bad feelings can cause us to push away all emotion, including our positive feelings, both of which are unhealthy. So to deal with negative emotions, first practice acknowledging your emotions. Doing that will help you in more ways than one. How many times have you gotten angry or upset at someone, but deep down you know that what you are arguing about is your fault? You know you screwed up, but you don't want to admit that to the person you are arguing with. Because of pride or ego, the argument escalates. You find yourself talking more loudly, saying things you later regret. What you're really doing is trying to cover up your mistake.

What's the other option? You could say, "You know what? You're right, I made a mistake. I'm sorry." Such simple words, but we don't want to say them. If instead we can acknowledge our emotions, admit the mistake, and simply apologize for it, we can put the episode behind us and move on. Not only that, but can you see how much energy, emotion, and potential negative consequences that saves?

In the same vein, we may have to deal with negative feelings about our past that arise. Sometimes we feel shame for what we've done or the background we came from. You don't need to feel as if you should hide the circumstances of your past. I had to clean toilets in a hotel when I first came to the United States. I'm proud of my first job. It was the first step on my journey to where I am now. When we try to hide things from our past, we end up spending more energy trying to hide them than admitting that they were part of our past and that they helped make us who we are. Again, it doesn't matter what you did or what circumstance you were in before. What matters is what you determine to make happen now and in the future. If negative emotions about your past arise, acknowledge how you are feeling and remind yourself that no one can hold anything against you or judge you if you don't judge yourself.

In reality, the fact that somebody is judging you is none of your business. What they are saying has nothing to do with you. It's about them. They are describing themselves as they see you through their own filter, as we saw in Teresa's story earlier. Many times, people who are critical of you are actually doing you a favor. Say you were considering this person as a friend, business partner, or mentor. Fortunately, they have now revealed their true personality and you can say to yourself, "Thank you very much for showing me your true character! You helped me make an important decision."

So the first step to dealing with negative emotions is to acknowledge your emotions. Once you have acknowledged the presence of a negative feeling, the second step for moving beyond that feeling is to keep in mind that you have three options for dealing with that feeling. Avoid the first two options and choose the third.

Option 1: Carving in Wood or Stone

Have you ever immortalized a romance between you and a girlfriend or boyfriend by carving your names in a tree trunk or in wet cement? The idea was to make the symbol permanent. Similarly, you may have already carved some negative emotional states, such as anger, worry, resentment, jealousy, fear, or sorrow, into your consciousness. Those emotions are coming from either your conscious or your subconscious mind. You may have felt so righteously justified in feeling them that you accepted them and had no intention of letting them go. But who does this really affect? You. It hurts only you. Of course, when you adopted those negative feelings, you probably didn't realize that choosing this option would eventually obstruct your growth.

Option 2: Writing in Sand

The Native Americans created sand drawings, knowing full well that ultimately the wind would blow them away. "Writing in sand" is how I describe negative emotions that we hold on to until something external happens to stimulate them or change them. We haven't determined to keep these negative feelings, but we also haven't determined to release them either. That is an unstable emotional condition because we are not taking charge of those emotions and aren't taking constructive action to neutralize them.

Maybe the emotions will be discharged smoothly; maybe they won't. But their presence, until removed, is counterproductive and obstructive.

Option 3: Writing in Water

We cannot really write in water. We cannot carve in water. Water's nature is to flow. That is how we should treat a negative emotion. When it comes, let it go. Let it flow away from you like water moving down a riverbed. Do not allow it to reside in your consciousness for any amount of time and do not allow it to become permanent. *Release the negative emotion as soon as it comes.*

"I can't," you may say. *"You can,"* says your Silent Master. No matter how intense an emotion may be, if you immediately refuse to dwell on it and refuse to focus on it, it has no staying power. Speed is the key. Act quickly to release it.

I want to make clear that releasing an emotion is different than covering up or suppressing an emotion. When you release an emotion, you don't deny having the feeling. You acknowledge what you are feeling but immediately let it flow through and away from you instead of holding on to it.

One reason you may not let go of negative feelings is that, to some extent, you may enjoy your negative emotional states. Be willing to admit that perhaps you've found them comfortable, familiar friends. Yes, on the surface you may say that it's no fun being angry. But are you sure? Are you sure you're not holding on to the negative emotion because you think there is a payoff, such as "When I'm angry, I like the feeling of being 'right'" or "When I'm depressed, my husband or wife pays more attention to me." Manipulating others through negative states is what I call emotional blackmail. If you discover that you are actually getting a kick out of behaving like that, think twice. Nothing good will come your way from putting out negative emotions to get what you want from others.

Capture the Positive Momentum

If you find yourself growing more and more uncomfortable with your negative emotions, if they are annoying distractions to the little flame of peace and well-being starting to glow within you, if you find yourself wanting to nurture even the smallest, most quiet feeling of self-appreciation, if you find yourself wanting, really wanting, to be happy within yourself, you are feeling your Silent Master. You have already met each other. Now you can know that this little manifestation of real feeling is destined to unfold into the whole consciousness of love, peace, harmony, and creative power.

All you need to do is harness this unfolding power, hold on to it, and let it grow. Then consciously work to replace your negative emotional patterns with feelings that support your goal, whatever it may be. Have you heard that nothing succeeds like success? That is so. Every positive feeling expands and creates more positive feelings. Capture this momentum.

Remember, "Your Silent Master expresses completeness, fulfillment, harmony, peace, joy, and love and imparts these qualities to everything it creates." Because your Silent Master *is* the consciousness of love, and because you *are* your Silent Master, love yourself! Lift yourself out of your negative emotional patterns with determination and total commitment.

FOR YOUR REFLECTION

1. The first principle of mental conduct tells us that in order to grow stronger and achieve our goals and dreams, we must be honest about both our strengths and our weaknesses. See how well you really know yourself by answering the following questions.

- What are ten strengths that I have? On a piece of paper or in your journal, list these strengths.

- What are ten weaknesses I have? Make a separate list of these weaknesses. (Be objective when doing this and do not judge yourself.)

2. List your ten weaknesses again. Next to each one, write the answer to these questions:

- What quality could I develop that would negate that weakness and turn it into a strength that supports my well-being?

- Are any of my perceived "weaknesses" really a fear to do something or express a part of myself because someone in the past has told me that I am not good at that or cannot do it? If so, what fear do I have that is based on someone else's opinion? What steps can I take to overcome that fear and turn it into a friend?

3. Negative feelings we hold on to may be in conflict with the valuable changes we wish to make.

- First, list the areas in your life where you are trying to make a constructive change.

- Now list five negative feelings that you have had lately, even if they seem to have nothing to do with these changes. Do not think about the negative feelings. Just write quickly whatever comes to your mind.

- Follow the negative thoughts you just expressed. Where do they lead you? Do you think they support the change you are trying to make?

4. Learning to be specific and to focus your objectives clearly in your mind is key to harnessing the power of right thinking.

- List a single short-term goal that you wish to achieve (such as "I want to improve my appearance").

- State it again, more specifically this time (for example, "I want to lose weight").

- State it again, even more specifically (how much weight do you want to lose? by what date?).

- Have you taken steps to reach this goal? What have you done? What do you still need to do?

5. Your Silent Master consciousness operates over both your conscious and subconscious mind and is ready to give you all the insight, information, and direction you need to fulfill your dreams, ambitions, and goals. You can ask your Silent Master a question, knowing the answer *will* come into your conscious awareness, whether it happens quickly or after some time.

- Think of the most pressing, difficult, or painful areas of your life at this moment. Write down the questions you want to ask your real self about them.

C h a p t e r   F o u r

Three Tools of the Warrior

You become a warrior—a warrior on the path of uniting body, mind, and spirit—as soon as you begin practicing the five principles of mental conduct you explored in the last chapter. Living by those principles allows you to take charge of your thinking so that your mental activity supports you rather than sabotages you.

Before we move on to the seven steps to inner power, I want to introduce you to three more tools that are essential for your journey: *balance, awareness,* and *visualization.* Just as a traditional warrior carries with him at all times the tools necessary to fulfill his role, so you'll find these three tools indispensable on your path to inner power and overcoming. *Balance* is the armor you wear so you can travel fearlessly through any experience life brings to you. *Awareness* is a shield that will deflect what you do not need or want. *Visualization* is the sword that will cut through worn, outmoded, or negative forms to make room for the new.

BALANCE

The Nature of Life—Unity through Polarity

What holds the atoms of this book together? What keeps them from flying apart and disintegrating this book? In the simplest terms of classical physics, the atoms in this book are held together by a polarized force composed of equal and opposite electrical charges called protons and electrons. In the nucleus of each atom is a positive charge that is counterbalanced by an equal negative charge created by the orbiting electrons. Each atom is thereby unified and stabilized.

This is one way nature manifests a great fundamental principle of the universe—*unity through polarity*. That principle is depicted in Eastern philosophies, including Jung SuWon, as the yin-yang symbol shown here:

The yin-yang symbol describes the nature of the life force of the universe and everything created by it. It is a symbol of the oneness and interrelatedness of all creation. The circle taken as a whole also tells us that the life force of the universe operates via two equal and opposite forces. We see these forces in operation throughout our material world. They also manifest in some form on every level of our life experience. In other words, we experience the manifestations of yin and yang forces mentally, emotionally, spiritually, and physically.

The white half of the circle represents the yang force; the black half represents the yin force. Although these forces are equal and opposite, they are inextricably bound together as one. They do not, and cannot, exist independently of each other. Also note that a portion of the yin force appears in the yang force—symbolized by a tiny black circle within the white half—and vice versa. You will see in a moment how this has great significance.

First let's look at a few qualities and concepts manifested by these two forces to see how they differ. Then we'll explore how they blend and harmonize in a complementary fashion.

YANG	YIN
Male	Female
Creative (giving)	Receptive (receiving)
Aggressive	Passive
Strong	Weak
Heaven	Earth
White	Black
Hot	Cool
Light (radiating)	Dark (absorbing)
Thrusting	Yielding
Day	Night
Open	Hidden
Increase	Decrease
Fullness	Emptiness

Looking at these qualities or concepts, we tend to see them as opposites. Rather than thinking of them as opposites, however, think of them as giving rise to each other. That happens in two ways. First, we can say that fullness gives rise to the concept of emptiness because fullness automatically, by one definition, means that which is *not empty*. So in a way, fullness automatically creates the concept of emptiness. As you go through the list, you can see that this holds true for the other pairs of words.

There is another way these qualities give rise to each other. Do you notice in the yin-yang symbol that the black half increases in size until it "flows into" the small portion of the white half? The white then increases and flows into the small portion of the dark half. This means that as the yang force increases, there is a point at which it can increase no further, and then it "becomes" yin.

Here's an example of yin and yang at work in your body. I'm sure you've noticed that you are able to be energetic and active for a period of time (when yang is increasing), but at a certain point you must allow your energy to turn into relaxation and quiet. Being relaxed and quiet is the yin state, and when that state is fulfilled, it flows into the yang state and you become active again. The states of yin and yang balance your energy so that you are neither dangerously overexerting nor stagnantly passive. So while you can think of activity and rest as opposites, it's more accurate to say that they give rise to each other, turn into each other, complement each other, and create harmony and balance.

The dot of white in the black, or yin, area symbolizes that the yin force carries the "seed" of the yang force within it. At the right time, yin is destined to turn into yang. The yang force likewise has the seed of the yin force within it and will ultimately become yin. That brings us back to this core truth: "Your Silent Master consciousness was born out of the infinite life force creating and animating the universe. You exist as part of the universe; therefore, the life force is what creates and animates you. It is the power that beats your heart. Because you are this consciousness, whatever qualities the life force possesses, you possess also."

Because the yin-yang symbol describes the life force of the universe, it also describes your Silent Master consciousness, which contains all the qualities and all the potential of both yin and yang. You have the capability to express either one at the appropriate time to maintain balance in any situation. A man, as a biological expression of the yang force, will tend to manifest the strong, "aggressive" qualities associated with it. But in a balanced state of mind, he is also capable of expressing the receptive, yielding qualities of the female, or yin, force when appropriate.

Your real self is a perfect balance of yin and yang qualities, and true freedom is the freedom to express the qualities of both. Unfortunately, many are discouraged from expressing the qualities associated with the opposite sex. In most cultures, many yang qualities have been assigned to male social roles and many yin qualities to female social roles. Yet in a confrontation on the job, a man has the right to express the quiet, receptive sensitivity of the female (yin) state without being labeled "weak." A woman has the right to express the penetrating, aggressive power of the male (yang) force without being labeled a "battle-ax." Appropriate action is always the key.

Your Silent Master knows whether a yin or yang action is needed to create balance in any situation. Thus, you must cultivate the qualities of both so that you can act appropriately. In the next section, you'll learn more about how to listen to your Silent Master consciousness so that you are guided into correct action.

The Rhythms of Change, the Purpose of Life

Perhaps the most obvious manifestation of yin and yang in action is change. The motion of the two forces of yin and yang in the world are seen in rhythms of change such as day and night, the ebb and flow of the tides, the changing of seasons, birth and death, death and regeneration, seed and harvest.

There are also rhythms of change in our bodies. Much has been written about biological rhythms, periods of increased and decreased energy that can affect our health and disposition. Some studies have helped employers create work shifts that harmonize with these rhythms. If you look carefully, you will see that there are also rhythms of change in other aspects of your life. Times of progress are followed by rest, followed by increase. Likewise, times of prosperity are followed by lack followed by abundance, joy is followed by sorrow followed by happiness, and so on.

Why is the knowledge of balance and change such a key tool? Because when you know that there are cycles of change, you avoid accepting limited or negative conditions as permanent or final. No matter where you are in a cycle, the seed for the new condition is there.

Just because that seed is present, though, does not mean it will automatically develop. Change itself is a journey, and at times it requires us to do some trimming and pruning, planting and harvesting. In the cycle of seed and harvest, for example, the harvest does not arrive automatically. The farmer must work the land, plant the seeds, and provide the water. When you desire a change, you must do the work of choosing to bring about the change and then support your choice with appropriate actions.

It's easy to want to change a bad condition into a good one and to make the choice to do so. But what about when a good condition changes into a bad one and you didn't choose that? The knowledge of balance and change is a tool here as well. That knowledge helps you keep your perspective when changes you didn't expect occur.

For instance, now you know that times of increase and fullness carry the seeds of decrease and emptiness—that after times of abundance some form of decrease may occur. You also know that this decrease inevitably contains the seed of a new increase, meant to give you even more than you had before. That knowledge will help you remember that decrease and emptiness are not necessarily negative states. They may be serving a purpose: to take away what is standing in the way of your greater good.

Thus there is another law associated with the laws of change: *unending progress.* This law affirms that the whole purpose of change and the whole purpose of continuous cycles of yin and yang is to take you higher, to make you grow, to give you more of what will lead you to a truer expression of your real self.

Your Silent Master, then, urges you to have an attitude of letting go. You needn't hold on to positive or negative conditions as though they will last forever. Rather, let the flow from yin to yang to yin lead you into harmonious, balanced, progressive change. Never be afraid of change. By letting go and listening to your Silent Master, all change should lead you into greater good. That is the purpose of change and the purpose of life.

AWARENESS

Hearing Your Inner Voice

I said earlier that your Silent Master knows when a yin or yang action is called for to create balance. Yet, how often do we find ourselves making the wrong move, increasing discord rather than eliminating it? You may even have had moments when you said, "If only I had listened to myself, I wouldn't have done that." You were probably right. You may not be aware of it, but your Silent Master speaks to you very quietly at times through the faculty we call intuition.

When you have an intuition, it feels like an impulse to say or do something that suddenly pops into your conscious mind. Generally, an intuition will feel like a right choice and will bring you a sense of serenity or peaceful resolution (even if you may not have wanted to do it). It may feel vague, as if it's not really your own thought, but it is.

This inner "voice" is actually your inner knowing. It is your Silent Master's knowing attempting to penetrate your consciousness with its truth. It does not necessarily speak softly; it only appears to do so because your surface thoughts and emotions noisily clamor for so much attention. Clearly, if you could consistently be aware of these leadings from your Silent Master, you could make the right moves at the right time.

How can you develop greater awareness of this supremely intelligent, quiet voice? Ideally, your awareness should be like a pool of still water. Light travels easily into still water, enabling you to see right into the water. However, when the wind blows and the water is agitated or when the water is polluted, you can't see clearly what's in it. The same is true of our minds. You can make your mind like a pool of still, clean water, undisturbed by turbulent surface thoughts, free from polluting feelings and emotions, so that the light of your Silent Master can travel easily into your awareness.

The first step toward doing that is to develop the ability to let go—to refuse to hold on to any condition as being permanent. In the same way that a river keeps itself clean by staying in motion, let negative thoughts and emotions flow away from you as quickly as they come. That takes courage and commitment, but don't be afraid. When you can let your thoughts and emotions come and go freely, you keep your mind swept clean of obstructing mental debris. How can you hear your Silent Master this very moment if your mind is occupied with yesterday's resentment? Or today's panic? Or tomorrow's anticipation? Or with fear, worry, and anger?

Living in the Now—the Only Creative Moment

A second way to develop greater awareness of your wise inner voice is to live in the now. Your Silent Master always speaks to you in the present moment, because now is all there is. Therefore, now is where reality is and now is where the creative moment is.

Why is now the only creative moment? When it was yesterday, you experienced it as now. When you experience tomorrow, it will be now. At this moment and every moment thereafter, it is now. It is never tomorrow or yesterday. What are you thinking right now? What concepts and emotions are you holding right now? Whatever they are, they are in the present moment and on the way to becoming manifest.

The key to listening to your Silent Master and creating harmony in your life is to live only in the present moment. Do you do that? Don't be surprised if in examining your thought habits, you discover that you never or hardly ever live in the present moment. When it is now, how often are you mentally somewhere else, thinking or worrying about what just happened or what's going to happen? Is your mental video recorder constantly playing pictures of the past and projecting concerns for the future? If so, you are giving up your creative power in the present moment.

True awareness means being right where you are, right now, without fear or worry or obsession about the future or past. When you manage to do that, a wonderful thing happens. Focused here, now, you become undistracted. You find yourself becoming mentally quiet. And when that happens, you "hear" your Silent Master quite clearly. You perceive all that is around you quite clearly. You find yourself knowing what to do—now, ten minutes from now, or tomorrow.

As a result, you consistently find yourself in the right place at the right time. Why? Because living in the present moment is an act of surrender to the greater intelligence of your Silent Master, the greater intelligence of life itself. In this listening state, moment by moment you feel and respond to its promptings. It is "guiding" you. We can also say that you and your Silent Master are moving together as one.

"But I have to plan," you may say. "I have to think about what I'm going to do ten minutes from now or tomorrow or it won't happen." Yes, you should make plans in the present moment. At the same time, keep yourself open to new incoming ideas that may change what you have planned. The point is to be aware every moment of what you are thinking, because whatever is going on now is on the way to manifesting. How important it is, then, to keep everything you don't want out of your moment-to-moment consciousness. How can you do that if you're not focused here, now?

So many of us go through our day on autopilot from the first moment we open our eyes in the morning. Many people are barely awake when they drag themselves out of bed, put the cat food in the bowl, turn on the coffeemaker, and head into the shower, thinking, "Oh my God, another day."

I tell my students when I am training them in present-moment awareness: When you wake up in the morning, don't simply drag yourself out of bed. Instead, pay attention. Be aware of your surroundings. See what's happening around you. Where do your eyes land first—the ceiling, your right side, your left side? On your wife, your husband, your pillow?

Ask yourself, "Am I happy?" Are you 100 percent happy or 70 percent happy or 40 percent happy when you wake up? Are you excited to start the day or dreading it? If you're only 40 percent happy when you have just woken up because you're feeling miserable or anxious, that's information you need to know. When you become your own "doctor," so to speak, objectively assessing your strengths and weaknesses, as I explained in chapter three, you need to understand how you are feeling in the moment. You analyze yourself in order to diagnose the next steps you need to take in the coming moment. The practice of being aware in the present moment has great rewards. When you can seize control of the now moment, you can take intelligent control of your life.

Sometimes the challenging times in our lives encourage us to be in the present moment and open to the truth within us. A challenge can catapult us into the present moment and the gift it holds. When my father would come home drunk at night, yelling at me and my mother, he would often send me out to get more rice wine for him. In my child's mind, I would wish he wouldn't drink any more alcohol because it would make the yelling and the beatings worse. I would ask myself over and over, "Why is he that way? Why does he do this every night? What is wrong? Is it my fault that he is like this?"

In order to get the rice wine, I had to walk through a field, where a special wild flower grew that bloomed only at night. Appropriately, they were called moon flowers. I was fascinated by them and would take solace in them. I would sit down in this field and look at the moon flowers opening their petals. "Why do you bloom in the night, beautiful moon flowers?" I would say. "You're not like any of the other flowers." Then it occurred to me that I was like those moon flowers, blooming in secret and having the courage to be different than all the other flowers.

In the midst of so much pain and suffering, I was able to open to that wondrous insight only because I stopped and allowed myself to be in the present. While I was communing with these delicate flowers, I forgot for a moment what my father was doing to me and I was able to drink in the wonder of life and glimpse the awesome truth of my own inner beauty.

VISUALIZATION

A Powerful Tool for Turning Ideas into Form

As I sat in the fields and watched the moon flowers gently open at night, I was also amazed that, even in the moonlight, their color was beautiful. I remember having the thought that surely our ideas of color come from nature. I thought about how often people look at flowers or a beautiful sunset and want to imitate those colors somehow—in art, in clothing, in many ways. Isn't it interesting that the purity of nature, its original natural beauty, inspires us to capture it or duplicate it? Certainly, that is one form of visualization—reproducing in representative ways what we see in the world around us.

Although ideas seem quite invisible compared to moon flowers or sunsets, they are as real and inspiring. Aren't you just as excited by a wonderful new idea as you are to experience something rare and beautiful in nature? In the same way that the world of nature inspires us to imitate its beauty, so we are naturally impelled to capture the beauty of true ideas in material form.

Remember that the true ideas that come to you are coming from your Silent Master: "Your Silent Master is your *real self,* your original self. It expresses itself through your thinking, through true ideas and thoughts in your mind." Those ideas are the primal, original source of everything that manifests in visible form. In fact, the word *idea* is derived from the Greek root word that means "to see." So an idea automatically carries with it the concept of visibility. Haven't you noticed that when you understand an idea, you usually say, "I see." In our universe, we turn ideas into material form. Visualization is a powerful tool for doing so.

Visualization is the process of forming a mental image. The process of forming images in our mind is also called imagining, something most of us do with relative ease. The word *image* comes from the same Latin root as the word *imitate.* This means that when we form an image, we are imitating, or creating a likeness of, something else. That something else is an idea. All images, whether those you see outside yourself or those you see in your mind's eye, are visible duplications of some idea.

Let's take the simple idea of "comfort." We can be extremely creative in turning that idea into form. What images come to mind when you think about comfort? Vacationing on a tropical island or sitting on a lounge chair by a pool? Getting a massage? Owning a certain kind of house or car? Being with a particular companion? Having a bank account of a certain size? You can see that comfort can take many visible forms. (I am talking about true comfort, not the sense of comfort that might come from using alcohol or drugs to escape from reality.)

Now, suppose someone were to look around and say, "I'm not comfortable in my life." What a strange and contradictory belief that is if you look at it closely. In the process of stating this negative condition, that person has actually affirmed the potential existence of the positive. When she says, "I am not comfortable," she is acknowledging that she knows the idea of comfort. And if she knows it, she can have it. She may have to work hard to make some mental and emotional changes to manifest it, but she can have it.

I use this example to show that most of your negative statements are exactly like this. "I am not financially stable, I am not happy, I am not healthy" means that you already know the ideas of financial stability, happiness, and health. If those ideas have not taken visible, tangible form in your life, you may not have used your power of visualization along with effort and discipline to support their manifestation.

Let's go back to the person who says, "I am not comfortable." She sees herself working at a job she dislikes and for which she is underpaid. She sees herself coming home to an apartment that is much too small and that has inadequate furnishings because she can't afford better. She sees herself going into debt to make ends meet. If you ask her to start a program of literally imagining herself in a job she wants, living in a spacious apartment or home, and having all the money she requires, she may become angry and tell you that that is impractical daydreaming. "Look at the visible facts," she may say. "I have to be realistic."

To be "realistic," however, is to know that all visible manifestations follow the ideas and images you hold in your mind. We explored that key concept in the last chapter. It bears repeating. You and the universe are inseparable. You are a unit; you are one. It is the nature of our universe that thought takes form. Therefore, because you are an integral part of our universe, your thinking takes form. The life force of the universe flows through you and beats your heart. When you think, you use its energy to create other forms of energy, and this energy literally materializes—takes form as matter. As the life force of the universe is creative, so you are also creative.

Part of being "realistic" is also realizing that the practice of creative visualization is not idle daydreaming or wishful thinking. It's important to understand the distinction. Daydreaming and fantasizing are undisciplined. When we are daydreaming, our mind is wandering here and there or we are focusing on unrealistic dreams.

It's not practical or a good use of our energy to visualize something that is a fantasy—that is unrealistic, wishful thinking. Real goals are realistic. It's unrealistic, for example, to have a goal of buying a second home in Hawaii that costs ten million dollars when you are barely making the rental payments on your one-room apartment. That's fantasizing. You may certainly be able to accomplish that someday, but your next goal and next step is something very different.

Practicing Creative and Focused Visualization

Creative visualization is much more than dreaming. It is *focused* imagining, with the power of your will and persistence behind it. It is an immaterial activity that takes form first as a mental image, then as a material image.

When you are practicing disciplined, determined, and creative visualization, you are engaging what I call your "future memory." Having a future memory of something is more than having a vision or goal. It is holding that vision with unwavering certainty. You are not 100 percent certain but 110 percent certain that your goal will become reality, because you've already experienced it as such. You've already planned it out and, in your future memory, you've already experienced it taking place. Now you are following through on the natural steps that will make this "memory" a reality. You "remember" your goal with the same vivid and sensory detail that you remember your first kiss. It is that real.

Making your goal a reality will take effort and discipline. I like to give the classic example of athletes who are preparing to compete in the Olympics. They have to be disciplined and they have to practice if they want to qualify. Likewise, you won't reach your goal with the snap of the finger or by ordering it for instant delivery from Amazon or eBay. It will take work and commitment. You have to approach your goals as if reaching them were a life-and-death matter. You have to be honest with yourself, evaluate the effort you are putting forth, and ask yourself, "Did I put in 110 percent effort today or only 30 percent effort?"

One of the things that helps you stay committed is that when something is part of your "future memory," you have no doubts at all about ultimately achieving it. How many times have you heard athletes say that they knew from the time they were children that they would be top competitors in their sport, whether it's a great gymnast, a tennis champion, or an Olympic gold medalist swimmer? When they were children, they already knew what they were meant to become and they practiced and perfected their skills to get there.

When my Jung SuWon students are in training and are getting ready to break a board for the first time, not only do they learn the proper hand and foot techniques to do this, but they also learn how to use their powers of visualization. They set specific and well-defined goals of what they want to accomplish and they engage their future memory. They see themselves at their qualifying event, showcasing every one of their new skills successfully. They see the people who have gathered for this event congratulating them on their success. They experience, *as if it were already a memory*, their great sense of accomplishment at having overcome challenges to get to this stage in their training.

The art of Jung SuWon, as you've learned, is the art of living life itself. It is training for life, not just training to perform on the mat. So I always teach my students to take the same principles they are learning on the mat and apply them to their everyday lives to overcome negative or limiting habit patterns, to improve their lifestyles or health, to reach their relationship or career goals. No matter what goals you are aiming for in your life, visualization is an essential tool to achieving them.

Visualization has been part of my own personal tool kit since I was trained by my martial arts master in Korea. He was the one who taught me to keep affirming and *seeing* that I could break free from the limitations of my culture and achieve my dreams to become a martial arts master and teacher myself. A few years after I came to the United States, when I was still pumping gas, cleaning bathrooms at the local hotel, and teaching martial arts classes out of an old garage, I nevertheless kept in mind my vision of opening my own martial arts school and dedicating myself fully to that endeavor. Each step of the way I used the power of my "future memory" to make my vision a physical reality, and with hard work and persistence it came to pass.

When I moved my base to California in 1985, I had a new set of challenges. I had to start all over again with a core group of students to establish a martial arts center and attract new students.

I had little money and resources at the time, and the rent was five times higher in California. But that didn't stop me. At one point, I was only able to rent a cement warehouse located in an empty field full of jackrabbits. My goal was to sign up enough new students so we could remodel the space. We would perform martial arts demonstrations in a nearby park to interest people in what we had to offer and then my team would give them a tour of our studio-to-be.

How do you get potential students and their parents interested in coming to an empty warehouse full of nothing but concrete to learn martial arts? By the power of visualization. At first, we didn't get much response because the parents couldn't understand how a warehouse could function as a martial arts studio. They were afraid it was a scam. So I walked through the warehouse with my team and painted for them a picture of exactly how this empty space would be transformed. I shared my strong future memory with them.

"Here's going to be the dojo, and there the kicking bag," I explained. "Here we will have the locker rooms and the showers . . ." (Showers were a big deal—we didn't have them at our facility in Vermont, and you can imagine how hot and sweaty everyone was after working out!) I painted the vision of our future studio with great precision so that my team could see it clearly in their mind's eye. Together, we shared the future memory of it.

That made all the difference. From that moment on, my team excitedly shared that same vision with every one of our visitors. The empty space was full of potential, we explained, and we mapped out our plans in detail, painting for our visitors that same vivid picture we were holding with unwavering determination in our own minds. In essence, we were inviting them to use their powers of visualization too, and it worked. By our grand opening, we had eighty-nine students and a special ribbon-cutting event with martial arts demonstrations. The mayor, the city councilman, members of the chamber of commerce, the police chief, and other local political figures came to our celebration.

Hold in Mind Images That Support Your Goals

You learned in the last chapter that it is important to be responsible when forming your quality purpose and determination, the fourth principle of mental conduct. Visualization is the first step in bringing forth your quality purpose, and you must exercise responsibility in what you imagine. The mental images you form must absolutely support what you want to create, and you should visualize them with as much detail and clarity as possible. If you give equal time to images contrary to your objective, it would be like trying to dig a hole and fill it at the same time—you'll make no progress.

Unfortunately, when we have idle time, many of us have a habit of running all sorts of negative pictures through our minds. Knowing that your thinking will take form in one way or the other, you can see that if you hold in mind an image that stems from fear, for instance, you are energizing what you fear. You are letting your fear put you in a prison of your own making. Knowing also that visualization is a powerful part of the creative process, you can use this wonderful tool to lend positive momentum to achieving your goals. Allow your mind to dwell only on those images that support you and others, and see how quickly things change. And again, when negative thoughts and emotions arise, let them flow away from you as quickly as they come.

Keep in mind, too, that if your ideas are different from what everyone else around you seems to be thinking, it doesn't mean that you're wrong or that your ideas are not valuable. Most flowers bloom in the sun and close at night. But not all of them. The moon flower is an exception. We certainly cannot consider the moon flower to be "wrong" for blooming in the moonlight. Each of us has our own purpose, our own unique contribution and exceptional beauty to express. With *balance* as your armor, *awareness* as your shield, and *visualization* as your sword, you have three powerful tools to help you break through limitations and access your inner power to make your goals a reality.

FOR YOUR REFLECTION

1. *Balance:*

- Unity through polarity is one of the fundamental principles of the universe, depicted in the yin-yang symbol. The complementary forces of yin and yang are in operation throughout the world and in our own lives.

- List five concepts or forces that illustrate the concept of yin (female, quiet, passive) and yang (male, strong, active) existing together in unity and balance. Be bold in your thinking and look to nature for your answers.

- In the first column below, write down three situations in which you would typically express a yang action.

Yang Action   *Balancing Action*

_____   _____
_____   _____
_____   _____

- In the first column below, write down three situations in which you would typically express a yin action.

Yin Action   *Balancing Action*

_____   _____
_____   _____
_____   _____

- Now, in each of the second columns above, list ways you could balance out your yang actions and yin actions.

- What did you learn about yourself?

2. *Awareness:*

• One of the steps to greater awareness is living in the now, free of fear about the future or obsession about the past, so you can listen to your Silent Master, who speaks to you in the present moment.

• What is something in the past or a concern about the future that you often think about?

• Do you gain anything by thinking about this over and over? If not, what can you do to let it go and move on?

3. *Visualization:*

• List ten things you want in your life that you do not yet have. (List those that first come to your mind.)

• Pick the one item from your list that is most important to you.

• Close your eyes and see it in your mind. If it is a place or a goal, see how your surroundings look, how other people look, where you are, and what you feel like—as if you are already living that reality. If it is an object, see its color and shape. Visualize its every detail. Write or sketch what you see.

• Sometimes we hold in mind images that are contrary to our goals. What sorts of ideas or visualizations do you have that go against what you want in your life?

PART TWO

The Seven
Power Principles

The Seven Steps to Inner Power

WE ALL YEARN to express the most creative, true, and powerful part of ourselves and to share that with others. You already have the power within you to do that. But, as you've seen, the conditioning of family and society can leave us out of touch with our natural self and our natural inner power.

To reclaim your inner power, the power of your Silent Master, you must first identify with it. How do you identify with this powerful part of yourself so that it becomes your "I"? Again, by thinking as it thinks and acting as it acts. In fact, you can think of the powerful Silent Master within as another "frequency" of your consciousness that your mind can attune to whenever you want and wherever you are.

The seven steps to inner power will enable you to do that and to bring the creative part of yourself to life again. You do not have to struggle to accomplish this. Your creative power will unfold and develop automatically as you begin living by these seven principles, because they will cause you to think and act as your Silent Master does. I call them "steps" because they are interrelated and, one by one, they build upon each other. They are, in essence, seven ways of thinking, seven ways of being, seven qualities or skills. Working with each step is an opportunity to polish another facet of the diamond that is you. In part two, you will explore how to develop these seven qualities, which are, in actuality, the qualities of your own Silent Master. First, let me briefly introduce you to each one.

An Empowered Way of Living

The seven steps to inner power are the foundation of the path to finding and expressing the real you. No matter how that path progresses for you personally, these principles apply to everyone. They are the basis of all creative power. These seven qualities empower you to think and act with *body and mind as one,* with *truth, purity, love, loyalty, sacrifice,* and *patience.* In developing these qualities, you bring your Silent Master consciousness to bear on each and every aspect of your life.

I teach my martial arts students of all ages, as well as those I counsel and coach, to focus on the seven steps to inner power by seeing them as a code of ethics to live by:

As a warrior on the path to inner power,
I will strive to merge my *body and mind as one* so that
I may discover the *truth* about my strengths and weaknesses
and work to attain *purity* of body, mind, and spirit.
I will learn to *love* myself and maintain *loyalty* to my goals
and purpose. I will learn to *sacrifice* in order to achieve
these goals and seek *patience* in my ways so that I
may ultimately become the master of my life.

Each step, one leading to the other, becomes an affirmation and a reminder of your commitment to become your most authentic and powerful self in the face of any challenge or obstacle. As you will see, you can apply these affirmations and ways of living to any goal in your life.

The first step is to bring together your *body and mind as one*. It's so easy to become distracted and unfocused. In order to dedicate ourselves to our life goals, we must learn to unite our whole being in this task. In the second step, we seek the *truth* in ourselves and in the world around us. We look at who we really are, not who others say we are. This introspection helps us discover both our strengths and our weaknesses as well as our real goals. As we glimpse these truths about ourselves, we discover what we want to change in our lives in order to become who we want to be.

The third step cultivates *purity*. As we recognize our fears and weaknesses, we build the desire to remove those self-limitations. Our goal is to purify our bodies, minds, and spirits from the negative influences we've imposed on them from our lifestyle, attitude, and environment. By identifying with and developing the pure qualities of our real self, we free ourselves to express our greatest potential.

The fourth step to inner power is to learn to *love* ourselves with a pure, accepting, and spiritual love. As we discover our potential, develop our strengths, and overcome our weaknesses, we see ourselves through our inner eyes. A growing sense of beauty and acceptance forms within us, ultimately leading to inner peace and self-contentment. The love we have for ourselves multiplies our self-worth and causes us to place a priority on our goals and development. This leads to the fifth step, where we develop an unswerving commitment and *loyalty* to ourselves and our growth—to our beliefs, our purpose, and our path.

Sacrifice is the sixth principle of inner power. Through sacrifice, we eliminate unnecessary activities and make decisions about where to spend our energy, time, money, and resources so that we can achieve our goals. We realize that we must let go of certain things in our lives—attachments, desires, perhaps even ties to specific individuals—because we see that they are unhealthy distractions that sidetrack us from our ultimate goals.

Finally, we develop *patience* with ourselves and others. We learn to be content with the path we have chosen and with our progress. We stop living for tomorrow and live and breathe the journey right now, weathering life's surprises and disappointments, remaining at peace with our direction and with ourselves. Join me now as together we take the first step on the path to greater inner power.

Chapter   Five

Step One:
Body and Mind as One

*As a warrior on the path to inner power,
I will strive to merge my body and mind as one . . .*

YOU'VE ALREADY DISCOVERED why it's important to discipline your mind to take control of your life. The first step to inner power reveals that it's just as important to discipline your body so that your physical actions conform to your mental objectives—so that your body and mind act as one.

Remember the example I gave earlier that holding negative visual images in your mind that are opposed to your positive visual images is like digging a hole and filling it at the same time? That is counterproductive, to say the least. In the same way, if your physical actions don't support your mental objectives—if your mind and body are not acting together as one in pursuit of your goals—you will sabotage your efforts. When all your physical actions support your objectives and goals, the opposite takes place—you gain momentum toward achieving your goals.

Your body and mind are designed to act as one at all times. They are different aspects, different manifestations, different "frequencies" of the same life force. That is why I often use the term "body-mind" to reinforce the inherent oneness of these elements of our being.

Our mind and our body may seem like two separate things, but from an energetic point of view that is not true. There is always only one thing, one universal field of energy, or ki, if you will, that remains one field even as it manifests everything within itself. Our observing mind and our physical body, though they appear to be separate, are one unit. When we change one, we change the other in some way.

The Distractions That Divide Us

Engaging your body and mind to act as one takes determination and concentration. For instance, say you have set a goal of winning a marathon race. Your mind says, "This is an important priority. I want to win. I want to use all my spare time building up my speed and endurance every day." If you nevertheless insist on eating improperly, partying all night long, skipping workouts "just this one time," accepting invitations to do things that distract you and exhaust your time and energy, and on and on, is your body at one with your mind? How likely are you to succeed under those circumstances? Clearly, if winning a marathon race is a priority for you, if you truly want to win, you will have to take control of your body and make all your physical activity conform to your goal. Your body and mind must be working together as one.

Say you are in college and have met someone you're interested in dating. Just thinking of her makes your heart beat faster. You say, "I can't wait to take this girl out." Meanwhile, you have an exam coming up and you need to study. You sit down, you look at your books, and you read over your notes for hours. Yet all this time your mind is thinking, "I can't wait to convince her to let me take her out. We'll have such a great time . . ." Your mind is somewhere else.

The next day, you take your exam and are surprised that you performed so poorly. "Wow," you say to yourself. "I studied so hard, but I didn't know the answers. What happened?" What happened is that you didn't bring your body and mind together to act as one. Your mind and your actions were on two different tracks. Your mind wasn't supporting your goals and wasn't aligned with your physical actions.

Here's another example. Say you are the best salesperson at your company. You understand your product, the market, and your potential customers thoroughly and you know your presentation inside and out. But what happens when your fiancé tells you that he or she wants to break off your engagement and wants to be with your best friend instead? Your mind becomes blurred, you can't remember important details, and your performance drops to your lowest levels ever. Why? You are divided. Your body and mind are not working together as one. Of course, it's natural to be upset when something like that happens, but if you don't get a handle on it and keep your obsessive mind from fixating on this for months on end, that huge distraction will drag down every other part of your life.

The Power of Total Engagement

To give you an idea of how powerful it is when body and mind are working together as one, think of a movie you have seen that was so riveting that you couldn't forget it for days. When the actors are completely engaged in the roles they are playing, we become caught up in their performance. Even though we know they are acting, we feel what they feel. We wring our hands, our heart beats more quickly when they are in danger, we laugh and we cry with them. That's because their body and mind, which includes their emotions, are moving together as one. They are so engaged in their performance that it becomes real to them and it becomes real to us. We call it a "powerful" performance.

To illustrate this idea further, let's look at two couples. The first couple has been married for more than twenty years and when they have sex, it's a very rote affair. He engages in the act for his own self-gratification, not really caring about her or her feelings. She just thinks of it as a duty. Maybe her mind is totally disengaged and she's saying to herself, "Hurry up, I've got things to do." Maybe his mind is distracted, too, because he's comparing how he feels with his wife to how he felt with his first girlfriend or he's entertaining some other fantasy.

In contrast, the second couple give themselves completely to each other—with their bodies, mind, and emotions. Their attention is only on each other. They are producing inner beauty through their intimacy, filling each other with amazing energy and sharing comfort, joy, and happiness. They are one in body, mind, and spirit, and the result is powerfully fulfilling.

Total engagement in anything you do gives you tremendous power and fulfillment. Every moment, you can make the choice of what you want and then train both your body (including your physical actions) and your mind to move in that one direction. Remember, there will never be a tomorrow to realize your goals. What you do with every moment of now is all that matters. When you know your mind and body are one right now, when you let this principle reach into every aspect of your living experience, you will be in the driver's seat. You will take control. You will be thinking as your Silent Master thinks.

Keep Your Whole Being in Balance

Another way our body and mind can become divided in our everyday life is that we get out of balance by focusing on only one or the other element of this dynamic partnership. Some people, for instance, spend a lot of time and energy going to the gym or running up mountains, constantly pushing their bodies to do more and more. They are in great physical shape, but they have neglected their inner world. They can't express their emotions and they don't have satisfying relationships. Inside, they may be lonely and empty. To take it to an extreme, sometimes people get so fixated on the condition of their bodies that that becomes their god. Exercising is not good enough, and they may decide to take steroids, which can have unhealthy consequences.

Other people may focus on developing their mind or their spirituality, but they don't take care of their body. You hear them say, "I'm meditating and I'm doing all this inner work," but they never exercise their physical body. So the condition of their body lags behind and they are surprised when they develop all kinds of physical problems. "I'm doing all this spiritual work," they complain. "Why am I so stressed out and sick? How come I have this painful back problem or neck pain?"

It's never healthy to focus on one aspect of your being and forget about the others. Your whole being wants to be in balance, like the yin and yang forces of nature. Many times, you can accomplish this with just a little adjustment. For example, the person who wants to meditate but says they don't have time to exercise can create some balance by walking as they silently meditate and finding ways to stretch and flex their body as they stop along the way. They can stretch their calf against a tree trunk or see how far they can stretch their arm to pick a flower or piece of fruit.

The issue many of us face today is that our twenty-first century lifestyle requires us to spend a lot of time sitting behind a desk or traveling in a car. But our bodies are naturally made to be in motion, not sitting still. To get the balance we need, we have to be disciplined in making time every hour or so to have some fun moving—moving our legs, our shoulders, our arms, our hands. You were meant to be moving and walking, and your body will be healthier for it.

Your body is the living temple of your consciousness, a manifestation of your Silent Master consciousness. It is a holy place and deserves your love, care, and respect. Your body is meant to be well and whole and to beautifully carry out the instructions of your mind like a faithful servant. By caring for your body, you nourish your mind, and vice versa.

If you continually divide your body and mind, one or the other will eventually let you know. When physical, mental, or emotional problems start to crop up, that is your "body-mind" saying, "Wake up! Don't separate me. Put me back together." If a condition manifests in your body, don't ignore it. Your body is communicating with you and trying to let you know that you need balance. When conditions in your mind or emotions arise, they are likewise communicating that something is out of balance—that something needs your attention so you can achieve greater balance and unity. By listening to what your body and your mind and emotions are telling you, you will gain great insight about yourself and what you need to adjust as you move along your path toward greater inner power. Are you listening?

For Your Reflection

1. Think about the activities of your day today and what you accomplished (or tried to accomplish) or think about a goal you are working toward in your personal or professional life.

- Did you let distractions easily move you away from your goals?

- Were your body and mind working in tandem toward your goals? Why or why not?

- Do you tend to engage in activities that are at odds with your chosen goals and intentions? What kind of activities?

2. List at least three specific strategies that will help you improve how your mind and body work together.

- For example, if you are easily pulled off course by distractions, what will you do the next time you get an email, text message, phone call, or interruption you weren't expecting? Or if you tend to neglect your body by eating foods that make you tired or if you are not getting enough sleep, both of which will affect your mind's focus and performance, what action can you take to be sure that you stay in balance?

- How will you remind yourself to implement one of those strategies the next time the challenge arises?

3. Is your body or your mind communicating with you (through physical or emotional symptoms) to tell you that you may be out of balance? What message is your body or mind trying to give you?

Chapter   Six

Step Two:
Truth

As a warrior on the path to inner power
I will strive to merge my *body and mind as one* so that
I may discover the *truth* about my strengths and weaknesses . . .

TRUTH AS A STEP to inner power is the process of self-discovery. As you develop the habit of acting with your body and mind as one, and seeing your body and life experiences as pictures of your thinking, you will begin to learn something important about yourself. Isn't that what we call a moment of truth? What could be more important than awakening to these truths: *What are my strengths? What are my weaknesses? What do I see when I look at my life? Is what I see a reflection of my truest self?*

Let's look again at the statement we explored earlier: "Your Silent Master is your *real self,* your original self. . . . It is your eternal Selfhood that exists apart from your brain (which is a sensory processor only) and the personality traits imposed on you from your environment." The key question that comes out of that elegant truth is "Have I created myself primarily with information coming from my real self or with information coming from outside of me?" In other words, have you shaped yourself with information based on who you really are or with misinformation that came from something or someone in your environment? The answer may not be clear at first, but stay with this question and be very honest.

In chapter two, I mentioned dependency as being one of the first concepts we develop, and I discussed how our early dependency on others may have caused us to conform to their expectations. Furthermore, the culture you are raised in also affects your self-concept. You would most likely develop a different view of yourself if you were raised in Africa rather than in France or if you grew up in Russia rather than India because you would be exposed to different religious, political, and social ideas. All those ideas shape how we see our place in the world. So isn't it possible that you may have listened more to outside sources than to yourself in forming your self-image and, as a result, lost sight of some of your real qualities?

Looking Beyond the Five Senses

Another factor that can cause you to lose touch with yourself, with who you really are, is relying solely on the evidence of your five material senses to tell you who you are. Your senses of taste, touch, smell, hearing, and sight are wonderful processors of sensory information, but they are not the source of your intelligence. They are channels for your intelligence to flow through so that you can materially experience what you create—and that's all.

Let's take a person who believes she is physically weak. Perhaps as the youngest child in her family, she was unable to defend herself against the advances of older siblings and consequently developed the concept that she would never be strong. Sure enough, her belief took form as a weak, underdeveloped body. Now, as she looks out through her eyes and feels through her undeveloped muscles, all the sensory information going through her brain says, "I am weak."

But is she? That's what her brain says, but it's not what her Silent Master says. The truth is, strength is one of the ideas in the Silent Master consciousness; therefore she can express that idea. The word *express* literally means to "press outward." That person has a right to claim the idea of strength as belonging to her and press this idea outward into material form, into a body that expresses strength.

The opposite of that process is being "*im*pressed," which literally means to "press inward." That is what evidence gained through the five senses does. Daily our senses are bombarded with all kinds of sensations—screeching sounds that jar us, unkind words that affect us, smiles that make us happy. Whether good or bad, these images and sensations from outside *impress* us with a feeling of reality, making us feel that we can't change things. This can certainly *de*press us.

Our day-to-day thoughts come from and are stimulated by our five senses, and so our conscious mind and our environment are therefore deeply related. Yet because all outside images were first created as thoughts, new thoughts can create new images. We can change things, no matter what the sensory information in our brains tells us. However, we are not likely to create new thoughts if we are easily impressed with images and concepts coming to us from outside ourselves and if we regard that information as the final word.

Your Silent Master wants to express its beautiful ideas into form. Therefore, no material picture is the final statement, because the material picture is not the original reality. Ideas are the only real, enduring reality. As we express ideas, they may take many forms. Ideas are the cause; material forms are the effect.

What does this mean for you? When you look at your weaknesses, your limitations, your obstacles, you're looking at the effects of incorrect ideas about yourself. When you *know* these effects are not the real you, you will think as your Silent Master thinks.

The truth is that the only ideas about you that are real are ideas that express beauty, power, dominion, strength, love, wisdom, clarity, and perfection—ideas in your Silent Master consciousness. You express your Silent Master when you look past the sensory information processed through your brain and look only to those *unlimited* ideas as the source and manifestation of your true self. As you identify yourself with these ideas, you will see how you can move from one stage of development to another, setting higher and higher goals because, in truth, you are not limited.

What Is Your Worst Enemy?

It's important here to revisit a concept I touched on previously and take it a step further. I said that it is necessary to recognize our weaknesses as well as our strengths. The second step to inner power, being willing to discover the truth about your strengths and weaknesses, is putting that principle into practice.

Martial arts students know that their training is designed, in part, to bring to the fore their weaknesses and fears so that they can overcome them. In my classes I sometimes deliberately create difficult or uncomfortable situations because I want students to see their weaknesses so they can do something about them. I want them to understand that eliminating their weaknesses will make them stronger. At times new students will say, "I don't have any problems. I don't feel insecure or weak. I'm only here to get some exercise." Then after a little bit of training, I hear, "Gosh, I didn't realize I was afraid of this," or "I didn't know I had all this anger and impatience inside."

Isn't life like that too? In our interactions at work, at home, or in our communities, we may find ourselves in challenging situations or relationships that expose our weak points. Those situations are, in fact, designed to bring up our fears or other limitations so that we can see them for what they are and realize that we can take charge and that our environment does not have to control us.

If you are willing to be honest, face the truth that is being revealed to you, and be proactive in addressing it, you will find that you can make needed changes and avoid unnecessary pain. Unfortunately, we often face the truth and see our weaknesses with clarity only when a crisis arises in our lives.

I've seen many times after a couple goes through a divorce that one or the other, usually the woman, goes through a lot of pain and introspection. The divorce becomes a spark that lights a fire under her. She may decide to start taking better care of herself or change her hairstyle. She suddenly summons the willpower to stay on her diet program and lose weight, or she decides to finally work on being less critical of others moving forward. That's all because the divorce spurred her into action. Perhaps the husband decides to get in shape and work out or he suddenly realizes that working late every night and on weekends destroyed his relationship and he vows not to do that again.

The point is that long ago the husband and wife could have faced the truth and worked on making those changes, perhaps even avoiding the divorce altogether. Hiding from the truth is what will destroy your chances for happiness and success. Facing the truth—without judgment, just as it is—is what will free you.

In martial arts training, we learn to answer the question "What is your worst enemy?" I believe that your worst enemy is always your own fear and your own weaknesses. Unfortunately, we are not accustomed to acknowledging our weaknesses. We treat a weakness as some kind of ugly disease. That is not a healthy approach. To go back to the analogy I used earlier, you have to look objectively at your own weaknesses as a doctor would treat a patient he is trying to heal. The patient and the doctor must first accept the fact that the disease or weakness is present before taking steps to heal it. The same is true with our emotional wounds.

Having weaknesses is not "bad," and having them revealed to us isn't bad either. How can we begin to eliminate our weak points—our fear or anger or jealousy or laziness or deception—if we cannot see and then admit that these habits are giving us problems? We have to open our eyes to the truth that these habits exist before we can start to heal ourselves and make ourselves strong.

Rather than criticizing yourself when weaknesses or negatives show up in your life, rather than turning away from them or trying to ignore or suppress them, look for the message they are bringing you. If your life is not filled with forms that are as pure and true as you would like them to be, be assured that these negative pictures have a purpose. The negatives in your life simply show you where your beliefs need to be examined, where your thinking can be corrected, and where you can take positive action to change your environment and the path you are on.

When you are dedicated to seeing the truth in all aspects of your life, you say to yourself: "What is it that caused me to get angry? Where did that come from? Does it go back to something I experienced with my mom, my dad, my best friend, a teacher?" You've got to be totally honest with yourself about past experiences that caused you to take on the reactive behaviors you see in yourself. Once you do that and acknowledge that these patterns do not come from your true self, you can take action. With your mind and body acting together as one, you can take one step at a time to remove those self-defeating behaviors from your life.

This isn't an easy, one-time process. This kind of self-diagnosis is like peeling an onion, layer by layer. I teach my students to have the attitude that they are learning something new about themselves and about the world every day. I have lived for many years and have had so many different life experiences and lessons, but I know that I am still learning every single day. When you stop learning, you are saying that your life is at an end, and that's a very sad place to be.

Don't try to cover over feelings you may have of being unfulfilled, out of place, or unhappy. Listen to them. Those feelings may be telling you that you are not on your true path. There could be many reasons why you may have taken a path in life leading you away from rather than toward your true purpose. But the truth and purpose of your being, as well as all the mental, emotional, and physical tools you need, are here right now in your Silent Master consciousness. Any disharmony, illness, limitation, unhappiness, or tragedy is an opportunity to open to the reality and strengths of your true self, to tap into your ever-present Silent Master within.

How We Keep the Past Alive

The idea that we must face the truth before we can overcome a weakness or limitation may sound obvious and even simplistic, but in practice it is not always so easy to be truthful with ourselves. One of the reasons for this is that we may have convinced ourselves that we are a victim. A victim, by definition, has no control over his or her life. When we believe we have no control, we find ways to prove that we have no control. We may hide behind our stories of what's happened to us in the past as excuses for accepting why our life is not the way we want it to be and why it will never change.

It takes dedication to the truth—the truth of our limitations as well as the truth of our innate strength and power—to stop moving through life as though we are a victim. Jackie's story is a good example of someone who quite literally saved her life by finally facing that truth.

A year before Jackie began coming to me for counseling, she had been raped for the third time. She had tried to take her own life more than once. She could not get beyond the trauma. Not a day passed that she didn't relive the rape scenes. Her distraught state of mind severely undermined her ability to cope with the ordinary day-to-day stresses of life. Jackie had been in therapy, but no one had been able to help her remove the ever-present fear and turmoil she was experiencing. She was referred to me as a last resort.

You may not have had experiences exactly like Jackie's, but all of us, to one extent or another, have found ourselves reliving episodes of the past that we can't seem to release. So as you read this story, think of situations in your own life where you may have tightly held on to past traumas and experiences, which has kept the seed of those hurtful experiences alive.

The first thing I noticed about Jackie when I met her was that her whole demeanor portrayed her as a victim. Almost everything in her personal image and environment reinforced this pattern. She had an empty look in her eyes. Her wardrobe was drab and unflattering, her hair was a dull brown, and her hairstyle and her clothes were unbecoming. She drove a car that never worked properly to a job that was boring and uninspiring. You didn't need a degree in psychology to see she was really depressed. We do advertise ourselves by our lifestyle and how we look. The images that manifest in our lives, as you've been learning, are all a reflection of what we think of ourselves.

I worked with Jackie for a month and couldn't get through to her because she was so locked into the mentality that "I'm a victim. I'm not interested in living. I'm just miserable. Let me be invisible." I knew I had to find a new way to reach her and help her release this negative energy. I had to do something to stimulate her and wake her up. So I used a method I refer to as shock treatment to get her engaged in the process of healing herself.

The next time she came to see me, I said: "Please remind me, Jackie, you were raped how long ago? It was a month ago, right?"

"What?" she said. "I told you, the first time I was raped was three years ago, and last time was a date rape that happened a year ago."

"Oh, I'm so sorry," I said. "I thought it was just a month ago."

The next time she came for her appointment, I tried again. "I'm sorry, Jackie. Did I say last time that you were raped a month ago? I made a mistake. Actually, I realized that you were raped two weeks ago."

"Two weeks ago? No! I was here with you. I came to my session with you."

I said, "Oh, I'm so sorry. Right. The last time was a year ago."

We finished the session and I could see she was confused and upset by what I was saying. In her case, that meant we were making progress. I was slowly getting through to her. The next time we met, I said to her, "I'm sorry, Jackie. You were raped yesterday, right?"

"No, not yesterday! I told you, it was last year! I don't understand why you are saying that. What are you getting at?"

I could see she was ready to hear the truth, so I came right to the point: "Jackie, if that happened a year ago, why do you allow yourself to continue to be raped every day? You were first raped three years ago, and there is nothing we can do about that. But three years later, you are still giving yourself permission to be raped every day—mentally, emotionally, and spiritually.

"The man who raped you has completely forgotten about it by now. Why do you want to invite him in again to keep terrorizing you and holding you hostage? You are giving that power to him. Because you refuse to move on, you're allowing yourself be a victim."

After a moment of stunned silence, Jackie whispered, "Oh my God, is that what I'm doing?"

"That victim," I whispered back, "is *not* who you really are. Take that power back, walk out of that prison, and bring peace to your heart."

Because Jackie had been unable to let go of the mental and emotional images of the rapes, she was keeping the damage resulting from them alive. By awakening to the truth of what was really going on, she took her first step toward transformation. She was now ready for the next step.

Change Your Environment, Change Your Life

Although she wanted to release the patterns of victimization and go on to a new and happy life, Jackie hadn't found the strength and didn't have the know-how to do this. I believed the road to recovery for Jackie lay in uplifting her energy by completely changing the elements of her personal image and environment. The third rape, the date rape, had occurred in Jackie's own apartment, and she was still living there. The energy coming from objects of her past were literally stimulating the constant memory of the events of the past. She needed to create a new energetic environment to stimulate a new mental and emotional outlook.

"Okay," I told her, "now let's work on changing your lifestyle."

"What do you mean?" she asked with some trepidation.

"You really need to move out of your apartment. And you need to get rid of everything that belonged to you when the rape took place."

"You mean my stereo system? I just bought it three years ago, and I paid a lot of money for that."

I was stunned. I looked her in the eye and said, "Jackie, did you try to commit suicide?"

"Yes."

"And you're worried about your stereo? It sounds like you

value your stereo more than your life. You need to give yourself a new life. You have nothing in your apartment but the memory of what happened that day. Why do you want to be living in that apartment and hanging on to the possessions that will only remind you of the past?" I explained to her that our environment and our possessions trigger memories, just as hearing a certain song brings up specific memories. When you hear a certain song or see a certain object from your past, you say to yourself, "Oh, I remember. I heard that song when I was with my first boyfriend at the beach." The memory pulls you right back to that time and place. We remember exactly where we were and what we were doing when we used to listen to that song.

"Why do you want to live in surroundings that continually remind you of those horrible events? There's no reason to keep doing that. And don't worry," I assured her. "We'll get you a new stereo."

After this idea began to sink in, I made another suggestion: "Let's change your appearance too."

"What do you mean?" Jackie asked.

"Let's cut your hair short and dye it blond."

"But I like my long hair!" she objected.

"Jackie, you need to be honest with yourself. You don't really like anything about yourself—that's why you tried to commit suicide three times. You need to see yourself transforming into a new image. Try changing your hairstyle. Try putting on some tasteful makeup, adding some color into your clothing, abandoning the gray and brown clothes you always wear." Color is a natural part of our world, I told her. "Look at the colorful variety of fruits, flowers, plants, and animals in our world. God created all this color for us. I'm not talking about looking gaudy and unnatural but using color to bring out your natural beauty and uplift your spirits. Just look at how many millions of dollars businesses spend to choose the right colors in their marketing, advertising, and office spaces. That shows how important color is."

Jackie was starting to see how the changes I was suggesting made sense and was starting to visualize how her life could change. We went shopping together for a new wardrobe for her that was more vibrant, and she decided to completely change her hair color and hairstyle.

Afterwards, as she looked in the mirror, she said to me, "Oh my God, I don't know who I'm looking at."

"That's okay," I said with a smile. "You'll get to know that person."

I also helped her find a new apartment. She bought new furniture and created a colorful and upbeat décor that was very different from what she had before.

When her makeover was complete, she admitted to me, "You know, I really like myself."

I have counseled a lot of people who have tried to commit suicide or thought about doing so. When I ask them, "What do you want to do in your life?" they will say things like, "Oh, I've always wanted to travel" or "I always wanted to take piano lessons."

"Really?" I say. "That's great. But how can you do those things if you take your own life? When you go through any kind of trauma, you must think of that as the end of a chapter. Give yourself permission to turn the page, to have a new birth in your body, your emotions, your mind, your spirit. Start planning and design this new birth. It's time to get to really know yourself and what you want. No one is harassing you or bullying you or telling you that you have to do things in a certain way. You have the power to take charge and create your life. You have complete freedom."

I suggest to them, as I suggested to Jackie, that they change key elements of their lifestyle when they are starting their new life. If you like wearing your hair long, I say, try cutting it short. If you have always decorated in yellow and bought clothes that color, try using blue. Experiment and have fun doing it.

One of the principles I teach is that energy from our environment impacts us all the time, but we can get so accustomed to the energetic quality of our surroundings that we aren't aware of its effect. You may have noticed that certain rooms in your home or in someone else's home uplift you or make you feel down. Certain stores or restaurants may make you feel peaceful or agitated.

All the objects in a particular environment are made of energy, radiate energy, and absorb energy. Furniture bears the energetic imprint of the person who crafted it as well as other owners or users of it. You may find yourself saying, "I don't know why, but I just like this piece of furniture." Many times, you are responding to the positive energy carried by the object, not just its aesthetic value. The environment you create for yourself can, in effect, pull you up or drag you down. It's worth asking yourself from time to time: "Is my environment promoting my awareness of my strengths or is it smothering me? Do I need an energetic change?"

Overcoming Fear of Change

Jackie was learning these energy principles. Moving to a new apartment and completely changing her décor was an opportunity to start fresh and create a new vision of her life. The physical changes she made encouraged her to make other changes too—to find a new, more gratifying job and to buy a car that worked properly. As she gradually let go of her past, she also found herself acting like a new person, being more assertive, more confident, more in charge of herself as well as her surroundings. When her co-workers noticed the changes she was making, they said, "Oh, is that you Jackie? You look so beautiful! That color looks great on you. Wow, you look ten years younger. What happened?" As people made

GARY PUBLIC LIBRARY

positive comments and smiled at her, that in turn energized her and made her more open to sharing herself with others.

There was still a final step in Jackie's process of transformation, though. She had to overcome the fear of being in a relationship. Understandably, she was wary of men, though that reaction wasn't based on truth.

"Do you hate men?" I asked her. "Not all men behave the way you've been treated. Let's work on opening your heart to create space for a healthy, authentic relationship. I know you're going to fall in love with someone and that person is going to love you deeply. Let yourself be open to that."

To make a long story short, Jackie did eventually meet and fall in love with a wonderful man. She is now married, has two children, and is very happy. Our journey in life, like Jackie's, is full of surprises. We aren't looking for pain and hurt, but we can learn to rejoice in the lessons of pain and hurt. That is what gives us our strength and freedom.

Of course, the changes Jackie made in response to her challenges weren't easy for her to make and she resisted them at the beginning. The fear of change is something we all have to deal with, even when we desire a change for the better. Although Jackie's old life was full of unpleasantness, it was familiar. Things that are familiar, even though they are unpleasant, are often more comfortable than the unknown and untried. Although she was so unhappy and depressed that she had been pushed to the brink of suicide several times, Jackie was still attached to the way she had been living her life and to her material possessions—the very things that were keeping her a prisoner of her past.

Jackie shed all of that when she took the bold step of facing the truth that she was the one who was prolonging her misery. She did not have to play the role of victim over and over again. She could summon her inner strength to become the person she wanted to be.

It's simply a fact in life that when you want to create change, you must be brave in facing the truth—the truth of your current weaknesses *and* the truth of your innate strengths—and you must be adventurous in taking charge of your life and implementing that change. Remember, having a weakness is okay. It's only when you ignore or deny a weakness and let it drag you down and define you that it becomes a long-term stumbling block. Is it time for a new adventure in your life?

For Your Reflection

1. Think about situations in your life right now that are challenging or that you cannot seem to break free from.

- What stories do you tell yourself or others about why you are stuck?

- Are you portraying yourself as a victim in these stories? Are you using these stories as an excuse for not taking control of your own life and moving forward? How?

2. What would your life look like if you were free from those limiting circumstances?

- Specifically what would you look like, dress like, act like? Where would you live? What would your surrounding environment look like?

3. Thinking back to the story in this chapter and the successful changes Jackie made in her life, what changes can you make to break free from old patterns or past events you may be hanging on to?

- List three beginning steps you can take to create a new reality in your life.

Chapter Seven

Step Three:
Purity

As a warrior on the path to inner power,
I will strive to merge my *body and mind as one* so that
I may discover the *truth* about my strengths and weaknesses
and work to attain *purity* of body, mind, and spirit . . .

YOU'VE NOW SEEN how essential it is on the path to inner power for your body and mind to work together as one and to uncover the truth about yourself and your life—your strengths, your weaknesses, who you really are, and what you need to let go of. Once you are honest about your weaknesses and how they are keeping you from living the life you long to live, the next step is simply to ask: how do I clean up my life so I can access my full power and potential? That's where the third step to inner power, purity, comes in.

Something that is pure doesn't have anything foreign mixed in with it. It is uncontaminated and free from what weakens or pollutes it. When we affirm the truth of our original nature and reject foreign, limited concepts about ourselves, we are expressing purity. In other words, we don't want our consciousness to hold "poisons" and foreign impurities such as anger, hurt, frustration, jealousy, and other negatives that are not part of who we really are.

Not only do these impurities create limitations in our life, but, as research shows, the stress those kind of negative emotions produce can take form in our body through conditions like high blood pressure, heart attacks, and migraines. Here again we come back to the foundational principle you've been hearing throughout this book—the pictures you hold in your mind, whether false or accurate, will eventually come to manifest in your life. *Whatever happens in your mind happens next in your material world and your body.*

Holding on to limiting or fearful states of mind, therefore, can restrict or distort the quality of what you're trying to manifest. So when you are working toward making a change in your life, you have to carefully examine your state of mind for the presence of negative qualities that could work against the very things you're trying to manifest.

If, for example, you're trying to manifest more money in your life to use for good purposes, but you're fearfully hoarding or withholding money that should be rightfully flowing out from you, you're setting up an energetic conflict. If money can't flow out, it can't flow in. It can't flow period. If you feel guilty when you have more money than someone else, that feeling also works against your efforts to make more money. When you are aware of these limiting ways of thinking, or "impurities" as I'm calling them here, you naturally seek to find ways to purify and strengthen your mind so it can bring forth the forms you desire in the purest and best way.

Another way of understanding purity as a step to greater inner power is to say that purity is knowing and expressing your true nature. It is letting your body, mind, emotions, and spirit do what they are designed to do naturally while supporting their functions with good habits. You are your pure, true self when your thoughts and feelings come from the purity of your Silent Master and not from the many limited beliefs you've been calling your "self." The more purely and truly your thoughts and emotions mirror the consciousness of your real self, the more effectively you can respond to any limiting factors or obstacles.

That concept may require a shift in your thinking. Since the innate part of you that has power and mastery is perfect purity, you won't be working to *make* yourself pure. You will be working to *eliminate* from your mind and environment the thoughts and emotions that are impure. You will be taking away what is not you in order to allow what is the real you to shine forth.

Cleansing Your Mental and Emotional World

We all have a natural desire to keep our bodies and environments clean. That's why we routinely wash our bodies, clean our homes and places of work, clear our desks, wash our cars, etc. Your mind is also an environment—the environment in which your ideas, thoughts, and emotions reside. Like your physical environment, your thoughts and feelings require attention, care, and purification too.

I often find, though, that many people treat their cars better than their minds, or even better than their bodies for that matter. We at least make sure our cars get regular tune-ups, good gas, and careful washing and cleaning, but we don't always pay attention to the quality of our minds—the quality of our thoughts and feelings. Yet thoughts and feelings are the building blocks of our lives.

The concept is really very simple. Why do we brush our teeth every day? Why do we take a shower? Why do we clean our clothes? Because if we don't, we know exactly what will happen. If we don't brush our teeth, we know that plaque and bacteria will build up in our mouths, we'll get cavities, or, even worse, we may eventually need a root canal or develop gum disease, which can lead to heart disease and all sorts of other serious conditions. And when we wait too long to make healthy habits part of our hygiene, it's hard to undo the harm that has already been done.

In the same way, jealousy, anger, criticism, laziness, and other limiting habits can cause us harm. So, just as we wash our clothes, brush our teeth, and take a shower, we have to cleanse our emotional world of impurities. If we let emotional toxins pile up, we will have to spend a lot more time cleaning up the damage that comes from responding to others with anger, jealousy, or criticism. Would you rather invest your time creating beauty and positive results in your life or creating a mess that you'll have to cope with and clean up later?

When something in your life starts to go wrong, if you are honest you will come to realize that your own thoughts and feelings are contributing to the problem. Say you aspire to be a successful manager and are the kind of person who is good at making things happen. However, because you are very focused and direct in your manner, without realizing it you may come across to the people on your team as being harsh and critical. Unless you can recognize that tendency as part of your character and strive to purify the negatives (perhaps by balancing your directness with more compassion and support for your team members), the veneer of harshness and insensitivity will prevent you from being a truly successful leader, no matter where you end up working.

Here's another example. Suppose a person suddenly finds that his business is starting to fail. Perhaps his employees have become reckless and unreliable, certain vendors are being dishonest, and he's not able to collect payment for services from clients. His first tendency is to think of himself as a victim and to blame and criticize everyone around him. However, he soon discovers that reacting like that doesn't improve the situation. Still thinking the problem is entirely outside of himself, he fires certain employees and sues his clients for payment. Yet his problems persist.

Although it is not readily apparent to him, the failure of his business is really the result of an emotional pattern he is holding on to. To outer appearances, he seems intent on being successful, but under the surface the opposite is true. He is actually afraid of success because as a young man he saw how his father's drive to make more and more money ruined his father's health and tore him away from his family. Unconsciously, our businessman has come to believe that success automatically leads to bad health and family conflicts. Operating from that mistaken belief, he is afraid to be successful and has therefore unwittingly surrounded himself with people who will keep him from being successful.

His fear is carefully hidden, like most fears, and it doesn't occur to him to look within for the source of the trouble. Yet he won't be able to achieve success until he acknowledges the real source of the problem, purifies himself of that limiting belief, and then allows himself to express the confidence, wisdom, and power of his true self that will enable him to be successful without repeating his father's pattern.

We all have within us fears that counteract our desires, and they aren't always evident to us. We have many layers to our being, like layers of an onion, and those fears may reside on a very deep level. Sometimes we only become aware of the core issues at play when a shocking situation arises and puts us face to face with our weaknesses and fears so we can finally confront and overcome them. That's why the difficult situations in our lives are indeed often blessings.

Releasing Fear of the Unknown

On our path to inner power, one of the basic fears we are called to break through and move beyond is fear of the unknown. Have you ever had the experience of knowing in your gut that you needed to say goodbye to someone or something in your life that was harming or limiting you, but you were paralyzed by conscious or unconscious fear of the unknown—fear of what might happen if you made that change? That's what happened to Ryan. He was in charge of operations at a small start-up company that depended heavily on their operations manager, Kori, who seemed irreplaceable but was nonetheless making life miserable for everyone she worked with, especially Ryan. He knew he should replace her, but he was afraid to let her go. She seemed so integral to the success of their operations that he thought they would fail without her.

"She has all the vision and information in her head, so we can't lose her yet," he told the CEO. "I'll just have to take the brunt of her bad behavior for now for the good of the company." But things only got worse. Kori began to emotionally blackmail everyone around her. Her way of dealing with questions about her work and progress was to scream back, "Mind your own business! Do your own job and leave me alone—or else . . . " Even though her energy was toxic to the entire production team, Ryan kept saying to himself, "I'll wait until this next project is over to deal with this."

Painfully, this went on for more than a year because there was always a "next project" in the pipeline. Things came to a head one day when Kori blew up at the CEO and stormed out of an important meeting. "We can't wait any longer. She has to go now," the CEO told Ryan. "At this point, I'm willing to take that risk. And, Ryan, you've got to look at it like this: Kori's leaving may very well open the way for better things to come. Let's focus on that."

After Kori was gone, Ryan couldn't have been more surprised at what he discovered. All this time, he had thought Kori was the expert who was holding things together, only to find out that there were multiple problems with her work that she had been hiding. Although this discovery delayed the launch of their new product, it was actually a godsend because their team was able to fix those issues before the new product went to market. While fixing the problems was initially costly, getting rid of the toxic energy and "purifying" the work atmosphere propelled their company to much greater prosperity. Not only did the team regain their enthusiasm, but Kori's replacement was extremely talented, efficient, and a joy to work with. Ryan grew in his skills, too, because he learned from this incident to trust his intuition and not to let his fear of the unknown stop him from taking action to end a situation he knew in his heart was toxic.

Are the themes in Ryan's story familiar to you? The lessons he learned don't apply only to business situations. Think about your personal relationships. Are you afraid to let go of someone in your life you know is an unhealthy influence? Are you scared to say goodbye to so-called friends who constantly put you down because you think you won't be able to make new friends? Are you tolerating abuse from a spouse because you think staying together "is good for the children" or because you are scared of being on your own and venturing into unknown territory? Don't hang on to cancers like these. Be bold and daring. Be brave. Don't let any negative situation take you hostage. Instead, purify your life of these negative influences by summoning the courage to face the unknown and create a fresh start.

Claim Your Time for Self-Reflection

We're not always aware of the emotional patterns underlying the nagging issues in our lives. One way to discover a pattern before it turns into a crisis is to take an honest look at what your life looks like. What do your relationships and your environment look like? Do you see lack of space, confinement, disagreement, lack of unity, failure, repeating patterns of conflict? Be willing to acknowledge that there may be a connection between the pictures you see and your fears, your weaknesses, and your expectations. Be willing to become aware of your fears. An emotional pattern like fear of success or fear of the unknown will go on creating one picture of failure after another until it is corrected.

You can always seek professional help to aid you in identifying and changing mental or emotional patterns. Your Silent Master is ready to help you as well. When you need an answer to a problem that is beyond your immediate knowing, turn to your Silent Master for guidance. Your real self knows the patterns you are holding that are obstructing and limiting you. When your mind is clear, you can hear your real self speak to you—sometimes directly, sometimes through intuitions, inspirations, or insights. The practices of visualization and meditation that I'll cover in this chapter as well as in chapter thirteen can help you connect with this voice of wisdom within you.

Making time for self-reflection is essential in our busy twenty-first century. If anything, the demands on us are greater today than ever before. When we get so busy, the important work of self-reflection and communion with our Silent Master can get left behind. But as a warrior on the path to inner power, you know that you are in control of your time. An effective way to make time for this important inner work is to start booking appointments with yourself.

When you have an important meeting, you clear your schedule. Other things may come up, but you dedicate yourself to it and it alone. Schedule a meeting *with yourself* and give yourself the same dedicated time. Claim this time as your own. Value yourself enough to set aside an hour to review and evaluate what's happening in your life, to reflect back, to look yourself in the eye, and to commit to what you need to do moving forward.

Maybe you will look back at your week and admit to yourself

that you made some mistakes. Maybe you will see that you could have taken more initiative in a work situation and that you need to express more courage. Be humble about these observations and plan how you will take action when you return to work the next week. Most importantly, being alone and giving yourself some space is a way of preparing to listen to your Silent Master. How will you know when your Silent Master knocks on your door with a message for you unless you put aside the busyness and noise?

If your time is extremely limited, you can always make use of the one moment of privacy most of us can count on—our shower time. Some of the most creative ideas and solutions to problems can come in the shower. I'm sure you've had the experience where you've been trying to solve a problem and it is only when you get away from it and are by yourself, whether it's in the shower or on a walk, that, boom, the answer suddenly comes. That's because when you are not engaged in the flurry of activity whirling around you, when you are able to empty your mind, you open space to hear the wisdom of your original self.

A Healthy Mental Immune System

Now that you've been exploring what purity means as a step to inner power, you may be wondering where hate, illness, greed, lust, revenge, and all other negatives come from if your real self knows and embodies what is pure—love, health, generosity, compassion, etc. In actuality, negative concepts are not ideas at all. They are the absence of an idea, the unreal shadows of something real. When you see a shadow on the ground, you are not fooled into thinking it has substance. However, you do know there is something of real substance nearby that is casting the shadow. In other words, the shadow tells you that there is something real at hand. Can a shadow of yourself exist without you?

Here, then, is some good news—negative ideas are substantially unreal, like shadows. When you experience them, they are only pointing to a real idea you are not expressing. This means there is really nothing standing in the way of your purity. Truly, there is only one reality, and you can make it your business to express it. You can fill the void of your negatives or anyone else's by forming the positive idea.

Take greed, for instance, clearly a negative condition that is self-destructive. Greed is the absence of the knowledge that you have the power to create all that you need out of your own ideas. Greed is the absence of the knowledge that you are complete and whole. If you truly *know* that you can have what you think, that you can have all you need, that you are complete and whole, you do not feel greed.

Hate is the absence of love. That thing you hate so much— isn't it true that you hate it precisely because it falls so short of what you love? "I hate him" means "I love certain qualities he does not express." Because you know that hating will only reinforce and perpetuate the negative condition, you can choose to fill this negative void with loving energy that envisions and therefore helps to bring about the positive picture. Fear is the absence of power. You can fill this void by knowing that in truth you are a powerful being who has the inner strength to overcome any obstacle.

Continue for yourself now. Ask yourself, "What idea is lacking when I feel sorrow, when I feel shy, when I feel angry, when I feel jealous?" Go down your personal list and fill those voids with the pure ideas belonging to your real self. That work is part of your mental immune system. Doesn't your body's immune system operate on the principle of constantly distinguishing between self and not-self, and then eliminating what is not-self? A healthy *mental* immune system works the same way. Your mental immune system is your mental purity and the constant attention you give to discerning which thoughts are from your true self and which are from your not-self (the negative and limited thoughts).

Filling your consciousness with images of perfection and purity does not leave room for negative patterns to exist and manifest. When the negatives express themselves in your life, be sure to quickly let go of those thoughts—writing them in water, not carving them in stone, as you learned about in chapter three—and replace them with the positive image you want to manifest. When a negative manifests, we don't want to "dance" with it. Instead, we want to dance with our pure, original self and allow its force to transform our negative picture into one of wholeness and perfection.

I am not saying that you won't experience the ups and downs of life. The nature of material life is that pleasure and pain, happiness and sadness coexist and constantly change from one to the other. That is the nature of this world. Yet regardless of which polarity you are feeling at the moment, your Silent Master consciousness is still shining with purity, love, wholeness, peace, and joy. Your Silent Master consciousness does not fluctuate between happiness and sadness, gain and loss, joy and sorrow. It is the eternal, unchanging bliss of your pure being, your original self. It never "goes away." But you can go away from it by refusing to be aware of it.

The truth is that all energy, all negative energy and all positive energy, is made of the one, pure original ki energy that is your Silent Master. So instead of regarding your stress as distress, you can regard it as your Silent Master energy in disguise. In other words, all distortions of energy, whether they show up as fear, greed, jealousy, anger, or anything else, are capable of being transformed back into their original state.

The energy that you're expressing right now—no matter how much you do or don't like it—is your Silent Master energy colored by your beliefs, ideas, concepts, and emotions. Day by day, applying the techniques you're learning in this book, you can go through the process of purifying, brightening, and heightening your energy until you feel consciously at one with your Silent Master—until you feel yourself flow into the pattern that fulfills your highest potential, serving yourself, serving others, drawing your life force to its complete and beautiful expression.

Let Go of Criticism and Judgment

As you become aware of the energy and emotions you want to cleanse from your world, take care not to get caught up criticizing yourself for the trait you want to eliminate. Please don't get down on yourself for having doubts or being impatient or angry. The fact that you are noticing these tendencies means that you are *doing* something—you are engaged in your life. As I said earlier, look at these weaknesses clinically.

When you are driving down a dusty road on a hot day and your car becomes coated in dust, you don't label it as right or wrong. You accept that this is something that just happens, and you make a mental note to get the car washed the next time you are in town. When you're in a car and it starts raining, you notice that your windshield is getting wet and then you turn on your windshield wipers so you can drive safely. You don't curse the rain and say, "Why is this stupid water getting on my windshield and all over my car?"

It doesn't really matter how you feel about the rain. Maybe you have been experiencing a severe drought where you live and so you welcome the downpour, or maybe you've had drenching floods lately and you don't want to see another drop of rain. Regardless of how you feel, you have to deal with what's happening at the moment. Getting frustrated and bringing in emotions doesn't help. In order to move forward, you have to stay in balance, be positive, and take appropriate action.

Life is a journey, and in the same way that you experience rough weather at times, so you'll experience fear or doubt or jealousy. That's okay. See these attitudes for what they are and, because you know they are holding you back, set about replacing them with confidence in yourself, gratitude for what you have, and excitement to be alive with a new day of opportunity before you.

When you want to put a negative experience or feeling behind you, it's counterproductive to sink into self-pity or look at what happened as a disaster—even if it seems like a disaster at the moment. If you can summon the courage to let go of the negatives and move on rather than letting unhappy feelings or self-criticism chain you down, you'll find the freedom to explore new opportunities. That is an important life skill and an expression of a healthy mental immune system.

If you are splitting up with your spouse, for instance, as painful as it may be, realize that this is opening the way for you to meet someone you will be much happier with. If you've been told you are going to lose your job, see it as an opportunity—perhaps to go back to school to pursue a new, more satisfying career. The divorce or the layoff isn't really a tragedy. It all has to do with your point of view. When you're in the midst of these things, you don't know yet what's to come. So you can't judge them as a mistake or a catastrophe. Instead, see the change as full of potential.

If a purifying change you are experiencing in your life was a long time in coming, you may be tempted to lament the fact that it took you so long to wake up and make it happen. Don't criticize yourself for that either! You can take responsibility for your part in what happened, but now that you've woken up to the truth (or been woken up by someone or something), be grateful for the opportunity to use the seven steps to inner power to make adjustments that will take you to a new level. Are you going to keep yourself chained down with regret or are you going to have fun and experiment in your new playground?

Cleansing Techniques

I said that just as we regularly cleanse our physical body, so we must cleanse our thoughts and emotions. Stress, anger, anxiety, fear, disappointment, self-doubt—these things accumulate within us too. Have you ever had to go without showering or bathing for a couple of weeks? Remember how invigorated and renewed you felt when you were finally able to get clean? It will feel just as invigorating to cleanse your thoughts and emotions. I would like to share two simple but effective techniques you can use every day to shed the negatives and clear the way for your real self to shine through. Having a cleansing ritual that you practice regularly will not only help reinvigorate you but also set the stage for the transformation you want to create in your life.

People often say to me that they want to change their lives— maybe to get in shape, eat healthier food, train physically, or learn a hobby—but they are not always willing to invest the time or energy to do that. They want the process to be easy and, if possible, have someone else do the work for them. With the snap of a finger, they want their transformation. It doesn't work like that. We need to participate in our own transformation, even if it's a little bit each day. To be honest, don't you deserve some time to be with yourself and work on yourself every day rather than being constantly enslaved by a busy schedule?

When people tell me they are too busy to do anything for themselves, I say, "Do you shower or take a bath each day? Great, start with that." I talked about using that time to clear your mind and commune with your real self. You can go a step further and use this time to engage your powers of visualization and practice positive inner dialogue to support and mentally cleanse yourself.

Your shower time is your time, a time when you can be alone with your thoughts, usually with no distractions. Here you are in control of what you do with your mind. Yet most of the time when we shower, we are on autopilot. We mindlessly go through the motions while our wandering mind is worrying about what's going to happen today or all the tasks on our to-do list. Instead, your shower can be precious time for some valuable work on yourself when you do it mindfully and with enjoyable visualization in what I call "the shower meditation."

Think of your daily shower routine not as a rote chore but as a special occasion. Treat yourself as special, because you are. Set the stage by placing a healthy glass of water or tea next to the sink. Set out a nice, clean towel and the clothes you plan to wear, laying them out as if you were getting ready to go on an exciting date—a date with yourself.

Turn the water to just the right temperature and step into the shower to begin your purifying journey. Imagine that you're on a lush tropical island, at a secluded mountain getaway, or in a favorite spot that makes you feel at peace. Close your eyes and visualize it in detail. Then see your shower as a rushing waterfall surrounded by beautiful flowers and birds. Gentle winds are blowing with a blue sky above. The falling water is clean, clear, sparkling with energy. As the water flows over your body, feel yourself opening to receive the fresh, new energy in the water.

Imagine that the soap and the shampoo you are using are purifying formulas. As you massage the cleanser into your skin, feel it removing the layers of frustration, stress, or whatever feelings have taken over and accumulated in your world. Feel the water and the cleanser washing away tension, worries, regrets, frustrations, negativity—everything that burdens, hurts, or limits you. Acknowledge exactly what you want to let go of: "Yesterday was such a stressful and frustrating day. I got angry because I felt that everyone at work was criticizing me. I felt dumped on." Whatever the feelings, whatever has terrorized you or held you hostage, now is the time to identify them one by one. Then let them go. Release them and set yourself totally free. Reclaim your right to be who you can be!

When you are burdened by other people's actions and attitudes, remember to keep in mind that their actions are usually about them, not about you. Acknowledge your own contribution to the situation, but don't hold on to the feelings. Let the feelings go.

When you shampoo your hair, release whatever it is you want to get "out of your hair." Let the shampoo strip away all the feelings and attitudes you've taken on that don't come from your true self. Let it cleanse all actions you may have taken that are now "on your head." Release these emotions and do not give them any more power. Feel yourself becoming more relaxed, more happy, more peaceful, more free.

When the water goes down the drain, imagine any ill will, resentment, frustration, anger, jealousy being washed away. Once you get out of the shower, those negative feelings should no longer be with you. Let this be a new beginning. In essence, you are experiencing a rebirth right there during your shower time. Bring your body and mind together and see the truth of who you really are. Meet yourself, see how beautiful you are, how amazing you are. Of course there is room for improvement. There always is, but that doesn't mean you can't love who you are.

You can also finish your morning ritual by setting the tone and intention for your day. You have cleaned the slate with this purifying ritual so that you can write on a fresh white page as you start your day. Ask yourself how you want to look, feel, and act physically, emotionally, mentally, and spiritually. Breathe, relax, and see yourself that way. As you turn off the water and step out of the shower, hug yourself and say, "I'm very proud of you." Communicate with yourself in positive ways.

The Creative Power of Your Words

When you have let go of negative emotions during your shower meditation and are making your first impressions on the new day, be sure to use positive affirmations. Let your inner and outer dialogue with yourself be filled with positive declarations about your true self. Instead of saying, "I am not sad," be sure to affirm positives such as "I am full of the confidence and natural joy of my real self."

It's always important to consider the way we communicate and the words we use, whether in daily life, in our meditations, or in our inner dialogue. One of the most powerful avenues of expression your mind uses is your words. Consider for a moment how you think. Don't you generally "hear" yourself think? You express your ideas in words, words that either play in your mind or words you speak out loud.

Words have great creative power. Your words can tear someone down or inspire them to be a hero. Your words can spur someone to greater achievement or get them fired. Since words are the creative carriers of your mental energy, treat them with great respect and choose them carefully with all your heart. Be conscious of what you are saying. If you have to, pause before you speak. Careful means "full of care." I encourage you to send your words out with extreme care because with those words you can start World War III in your relationships. We've all had the experience of saying something we didn't mean and finding that the words, once released, go right ahead and have an effect, maybe one we didn't intend.

It's not so much the word itself that has an effect but the energy and vibration the word carries as you say it—your intent. The energy and intent you put behind your words makes all the difference. So when you're speaking to others as well as to yourself, examine what energy you are letting your words carry. Are you building up your ego in a selfish way that hurts others or are you boosting another's self-image? If a woman keeps telling her husband how stupid he is, he can start to believe that and decide that "if I can't do anything right, why bother trying at all?" In your dialogue with others and in your own inner dialogue, constantly reflect on whether you are paralyzing yourself and others or whether you are elevating yourself and others.

The concept of inner dialogue and talking with yourself may be new to you. I want to be sure you understand that when you say, "I am confident," "I am beautiful," "I am talented," you are not saying those things out of arrogance. You are saying them with an intent to reflect the truth—to reflect the real you. You have to bring out the courage to do that no matter what names people are calling you. I've been called many names over the years—"you are a curse, you are bad luck, you are a tomboy, you don't have the right-shaped eyes, you are a disaster." I had to constantly replace that with: "I am beautiful, I am amazing, I am one of a kind, I am petite (and it's okay to be petite), I am going to do something special with my life."

In addition, practice being alert to the effect other people's words could have on you *before* you let them into your world. You don't have to accept every word that is spoken to you. Be aware of the mental intent behind someone's words and decide if you will let that energy in or not.

When you are confronted with negativity or situations arise where you need to calm down or you need an infusion of energy, you can use a ritual similar to the shower meditation to cleanse yourself of the effects of the environment or your own or others' negative emotions. Say you have to make an important presentation at work, you are competing to get a job, or you have to confront someone who has been spreading lies about you. You're a nervous wreck, your mouth is dry, your hands are shaking, your feet are tapping restlessly. In cases like this where you need help on the spot, you can take what I call an "energy shower," which works at energetic levels.

First, rub your hands together until you've created the sensation of heat in your hands. Then take a deep breath in and out as you gently "cleanse" yourself, moving your hands in a circular, scrubbing action around and down your head and then all around your body. As you do this, see the negatives being cleansed away and removed, bringing you calm and peace. You can also go to the restroom and wash your hands, making use of the cleansing water element. Rinse out your mouth with water to counteract the dry mouth that nervousness can bring.

Techniques like these can create mental and emotional purification any time you need it. As you become more conscious of the quality of your thoughts and feelings and begin to use techniques like the ones you've learned about here, layer by layer you will be stripping away all that is not a part of the real you, allowing your bright, original self to shine through all you say and do.

1. You discovered in this chapter that when you experience negative ideas, they are in reality pointing to real ideas you are not expressing. You can fill the void of those negatives by forming positive ideas to replace them.

- List the ten weaknesses you wrote down in the exercise at the end of chapter three. For each one, describe the real idea you are not expressing. Here are two examples:

Weakness	*Unexpressed Real Idea*
Greed	I have the power to create all I need out of my own ideas.
Fear	My true self has the inner strength and power to face any challenge or obstacle.

- For each "unexpressed real idea," list an action you will take to express that idea and eliminate the weakness.

2. When you shower each day, you can experiment with using that time to mindfully cleanse your mind and emotions, re-create yourself, and set your intentions for the day with the shower meditation.

- What feelings (such as tension, regret, worry, fear) will you release and visualize being washed down the drain?

- Knowing that it's best to communicate with yourself using positive affirmations rather than naming negative emotions, what will you say to yourself while engaging in your daily shower meditation to reinforce the cleansing, purifying action you see taking place?

For example, instead of "I am not sad" or "I am free from fear and worry," you could say: "I am full of confidence in my inner power and the natural joy of my real self" or "I am a warrior. I will not be a victim. I will rise up and take charge of my life."

3. Are there ever circumstances in your day where you could benefit on the spot from using the "energy shower" technique described on page 177 to calm yourself, give yourself an infusion of energy, or eliminate unwanted stress, nervousness, or emotional energies?

• In what kind of situations could you use this technique?

Chapter Eight

Step Four:
Love

As a warrior on the path to inner power,
I will strive to merge my *body and mind as one* so that
I may discover the *truth* about my strengths and weaknesses
and work to attain *purity* of body, mind, and spirit.
I will learn to *love* myself . . .

WE USE THE WORD *LOVE* in so many different ways. "Oh, I love these flowers," we say. "I love that sunset," "I love your hairstyle," "I love the way that new app works." We say, "I love you," to our children, our spouses, our pets. But how often do we express love for ourselves and for who we are right now?

How often do you say to yourself, "You know what? That was a hard day. I'm proud of you for hanging in there. You did a really good job!" Or have you become an expert at criticizing yourself? Do you hear yourself saying every time you make even the smallest mistake, "Why can't you ever do anything right? You're so stupid!"

What kind of energy are you pumping into yourself daily? Hatred? Criticism? Disrespect? Or love?

It's a simple truth that before you can express love, you must know love—and before you can love another, you must first love yourself. You cannot share what you have not experienced. Yet many of us never learned about the concept of self-love growing up and we don't know how to love ourselves. Many people tell me that they always thought of love as being between two people. They are used to looking for love outside of themselves, always wondering, "Does she love me?" or "What can I do to make him love me more?" They have no idea what self-love is. "How can you have a relationship *with yourself*?" they ask. Let's start with understanding what love really is.

Love and all feelings of love come with recognizing what is true—what is true about yourself and everything around you. When you recognize and experience the truth about yourself, appreciating the pure qualities that are part of your original nature, you automatically feel love. You have a special feeling of happiness that is not dependent on anyone or anything because it comes *from* you, not to you from outside sources. From that pure love is born self-respect, self-esteem, and self-confidence.

In chapter two, we explored the concept that your original self "expresses completeness, fulfillment, harmony, peace, joy, and love, and imparts these qualities to everything it creates." Never forget that your original self, the Silent Master within you, is the same life force that created the universe. That life force is pure love. Everything it creates expresses love. That love may become temporarily clouded over, but it can never be destroyed. It is always there, even when we don't feel it. When it is clouded over with negative emotions or painful situations, this pure love keeps on loving until harmony is reached again. It is love that moves us from one stage of development to the next, transforming us as we discover more of our true self within.

Love Is Practical

We especially need to magnify the love we give ourselves when we are in a difficult situation, when we are being criticized, belittled, or abused. We may complain about hardships in our lives, but those difficulties can, in fact, help us generate greater love for ourselves. I had to lean on my own self-love and my own self-respect growing up because there were not very many people giving me love or respect. It was either that or go down under the weight of that pressure.

When you are faced with challenges from people who are trying to change who you are or who want to stop you from doing what you love, you can either use those circumstances to strengthen your self-love or let that self-love shrink and shrivel inside of you until you barely know it's there. If you are going to break through to the real you, you have to keep the spark of love alive.

That day as a young girl when my mother beat me and called me all kinds of names, and then grabbed the scissors and cut my hair very short to embarrass me so I wouldn't dare leave the house to practice martial arts, was a decisive moment for me. Yes, I was upset and embarrassed. Yes, I curled up in the corner and cried. But then I asked myself if all the things she was saying about me were really true. "No," I thought. "I am not that bad. I just want to learn martial arts and do something different with my life. What is wrong with that?" So I once again snuck out of the house and went right back to training.

It was love that kept me going through all the hardships. My family wanted me to conform to their vision for my life, but the love I felt inside of me was stronger than all the pressure coming from outside of me. My dreams and goals were bigger than their desire to hold me back.

This is where the power of choice comes in. I wouldn't let anyone rob me of my life or steal my dreams. You cannot let anyone rob you of your life or steal your dreams. In order to keep my dream of becoming a martial artist alive, I had to keep the spark of love and respect for myself alive. Those early experiences also taught me that we can choose to see every challenge in life as a motivator—as a coach who pushes and prods us to practice, practice, practice strengthening our ability to tap into the love inside of ourselves and stand up for our own truth.

Loving yourself, then, is not just an emotion. It is practical. On the path to inner power we have to get to know and love our whole self, and that includes our body. When you really love yourself, you care for your body. When you really love yourself, you do those things that help you maintain and build your energy and life force, not tear it down. You need to keep your physical body healthy and in balance so you can have a strong vehicle through which to fully express your inner power. Your body can take a lot of abuse, whether from unhealthy food, overwork, lack of sleep, or putting too much alcohol or chemicals into it. But if that's how you treat yourself, your body will wear out long before it should.

You can correct those imbalances lovingly and with sensitivity and compassion for what your body needs or you can pretend you don't hear the warning signs. You might say, "Oh, I've been so tired lately and I have so much to get done. I need to push harder. I'll have to find a pick-me-up to get through the day." So you decide to take in more caffeine, however you can get it. On top of your daily rounds of coffee, you start having an energy drink in the afternoon. When that's not enough, you find yourself drinking four, five, six energy drinks a day. You've seen the news stories about the dangers of drinking too many energy drinks—stress, insomnia, anxiety, high blood pressure, even cardiac arrest. But in your drive to keep going, you decide to ignore those warnings and go on abusing your body. Is that loving yourself?

If someone else forced you to drink a substance that endangered your health, you would call that abuse, wouldn't you? How is it any different when you do this to yourself? This example may be extreme, but you get the idea. Ask yourself how you treat your own body—with loving self-care or abuse? I am emphasizing this point because without a healthy body, you really cannot accomplish anything in life. When your body stops functioning, you stop living. So practice love by appreciating your body, loving your body, and treating it with care so you can continue to share your love and your gifts with others.

The Power of Practicing Gratitude

One way to express greater love and bring about the changes you desire in your life is to practice gratitude. That's because when you express gratitude, or appreciation, you are acknowledging that something good exists. That action energizes that good thing and gives it momentum to continue existing. So by consciously making gratitude part of your everyday life, you are energizing the good you want to attract. What do you have that you want to keep or what good thing do you want to attract into your life? Whatever it is, consciously express gratitude for it. That keeps it alive and vibrating in your experience. Gratitude lends more energy to it, giving it more momentum to materialize in your life.

When my mother beat me and cut my hair to embarrass me, gratitude was another factor that helped me through that experience—gratitude for my master, who was teaching me and training me in the ancient martial arts. He was the one who believed in me and supported me. My gratitude for his presence in my life filled my heart with love and kept me motivated.

Gratitude, as a powerful expression of love, can be one of the best transformational tools in your toolkit, and one of the easiest to use. Gratitude is simply the process of recognizing what is true. It is an act of awareness. I'll give you a small example of what I mean.

Once I was driving west along the highway into a magnificent sunset. The entire sky seemed like it was on fire with amazingly bright, burning colors: purple, orange, red, yellow, blue, pink. I had never seen so many colors in one place. Finding my vision restricted by the car windows, I pulled over at the next exit and got out so I could have a full view of this incredible sunset. After a few moments I began to notice cars rushing by. Some were filled with people talking to each other. In another, a man was using his mobile phone. In another, someone was trying to read a paper while keeping one eye on the road. I was puzzled because not everyone was aware of the magnificent sight in front of them. Most people seemed distracted in one way or another.

The feelings I experienced with the sunset—the great peace, joy, appreciation, and love that welled up—seemed to exist only for me at that moment. Of course, this sunset offered the opportunity for wonderful feelings to everyone else driving on this road, but only those who were willing to acknowledge the sunset—to consciously recognize its presence—would feel the impact of its beauty.

Gratitude, then, is the act of recognizing an idea or quality; and when you do so, you identify with it. When you identify with a true idea through gratitude, you feel the force of the love it contains. Feeling this love, you send it out again as greater, expanding gratitude. Then before you know it, your love is growing to appreciate more and more of the world around you—people, wildlife, nature, events. Ultimately, your consciousness *becomes* love, which you feel and express and which comes back to you everywhere in every way as beauty, harmony, and peace. When you express gratitude, you are connecting with the universal love that is your Silent Master consciousness.

You can practice gratitude from the moment you awake in the morning. As you open your eyes and look around, as you wiggle your toes and stretch your arms, are you grateful that you have the use of your eyes, your legs, your hands? Have you ever broken your leg or your arm? I have broken both, and I know how inconvenient it is. I couldn't even pull up a zipper. When you can't move your arm for a period of weeks or months, you can't wait to use your whole body again. You come to appreciate all the little things you were once able to do.

When you wake up and move your body before you begin your morning routine, pause for a moment to be grateful and happy for another day of opportunity. Think how blessed you are to have the use of your body. Celebrate, hum, sing as you stretch. Say, "Wow! I'm alive. Thank you for my hands, thank you for my feet, thank you for my eyes! I can see and touch, and what I see and feel is amazing."

I like to tell my students to greet every day as if they are preparing for a date with themselves. When you go out on a date, don't you pay more attention to how you look? You also have a feeling of anticipation and excitement for what it's going to be like. That's how your whole life can be. You can prepare for the day, for instance, by making sure your clothes and your hair look good, by making sure you have gotten enough sleep and eaten properly. You do all of that because you are making a commitment to yourself. You want to bring your best to the day. Why does that have to happen only when you are planning something special? Don't you want to treasure every day of your life? Don't you want to show up as your best self every single day?

Oftentimes when I go out for the day, I am so grateful for another day of opportunity that I prepare for it as if it is my wedding day or my birthday celebration or my final day on this earth. I pay attention to how I dress and look as if it is the most important day in my life, and I strive to be a positive force in the lives of those around me. We all have a choice for how we are going to live each day.

In addition to greeting each day with appreciation and anticipation, another way to grow the power of gratitude is to get into the habit of expressing thanks for the simplest gifts that come your way. When it rains and the next day you see the flowers growing so beautifully and the streams and rivers filling with water, you can practice gratitude by saying, "Thank you for sending this beautiful rain!" Love and gratitude are part of the natural interplay of giving and receiving. If we receive something from the universe or another person but don't express gratitude, we are takers only. Whenever we receive, we should naturally become a giver and in turn show our gratitude.

Think of gratitude as you would any other skill you want to master in life. As you've heard me say before, professional athletes are good at what they do because they constantly practice to improve and be at the top of their game. And their efforts also inspire and encourage their teammates. What about you? Are you consciously practicing the qualities you want to develop, including gratitude? Believe me, the more you practice gratitude, the better you will get at it and the more you will be able to energize the people around you.

You can express gratitude to others when you praise them, when you give generously, when you are affectionate, when you admire, when you cooperate, when you laugh, when you create something beautiful, when you share your true self with others. It doesn't cost you anything to say a kind word or to be compassionate or show your support. That is a blessing you can give from your heart.

Simply saying, "Thank you so very much for what you did the other day" or "What you did really made me happy" can make a huge difference in someone's life and in your day-to-day interactions. And don't assume that others know how you feel. Sometimes we don't go out of our way to say thank you because we think, "Well, they know what I'm thinking. They know I appreciate what they did." That's not always the case. The people in your life need to hear it directly from you. Try expressing more gratitude and see how that lifts your energy and the energy of the people you interact with.

I have shared here some of my suggestions for exercising more love and self-love in your life, but you will also have your own way of loving yourself and showing gratitude. Again, each of us is unique, so there is no one definition of how to love and care for yourself or what constitutes a loving response. There is no firm set of rules about how to love yourself. You can't compare yourself with anyone else, and you can't compare your choices with anyone else's choices. Every choice you make has to start with you and what's true for you.

You can determine each day, then, to get to know yourself a little better and get to know what's true for you—and have fun doing it. You can live with a sense of excitement, wonder, and gratitude. Nobody is going to charge you more taxes for being happy. Appreciate every day you are given as an occasion to learn to love— to love who you are, to love others, to connect with your authentic self. You have an opportunity each day to fall in love with the real you, to get to know who you are—your body, your hands, your feet, your eyes, your heart, your entire being—inside and out.

Loving through Every Difficulty

Even though I wake up grateful and excited about how my day will unfold and look forward to the plans I have for the day, I know things won't always go as I want them to. Sometimes a meeting is canceled, sometimes the weather is bad, sometimes unexpected events come up. But when you're expressing gratitude for your life and feel the excitement of experiencing the opportunities in each moment, you know that everything has a reason and is happening just for you. Without a life of gratitude, we forget that truth. Instead, we end up feeling miserable and thinking of ourselves as victims. We become passive and don't take control of our lives. We forget to keep our eyes open for the next opportunity that is around the corner.

The powerful presence of love within you desires above all to help you achieve your highest potential. It is love that brings you every situation, every obstacle, and every lesson as opportunities to create your greatest growth. Through every challenging circumstance we must still continue to accept and love ourselves. When we don't, our lack of self-love and self-acceptance can become a major chink in our armor.

Look at Elvis Presley, Michael Jackson, Prince, and any number of celebrities who were believed to have died from drug abuse. Everyone else thought they were at the top of their game, that they had everything they could ever want, that they were unbeatable. But, for any number of reasons, they didn't have true self-love. They were missing something essential in their lives.

Why would someone who seems to have it all turn to substance abuse? Often it's to escape the truth. They can't accept who they really are, weaknesses and all, which, as you know, is the second step to inner power. They haven't learned that everything in life is part of our journey and that just because we see weaknesses in ourselves does not mean we are any less lovable. When you understand how love works, you know that everything you are seeing and facing within yourself as well as everything that is happening around you is there to ultimately create good if you use it as a stepping-stone to greater inner power.

Of course, love as a step to inner power does not refer only to loving yourself. It means loving others as well as yourself unconditionally. Love will never reach its full potential unless you turn around and share it with others. It doesn't really bloom to its fullest until you can complete the circle by giving love to others. True love has no "conditions" placed on its expression. You simply remain true to yourself with everyone, and give your best to them. *What more can there be to love than being true to yourself and giving your truth everywhere to everyone?*

Because love is real and true, it is powerful. It can overcome anything untrue simply by being there, just as the sunlight burns away clouds. As an example, one of my students had to visit someone who had once tried to take violent action against him. He was naturally scared to go to the meeting and talked to me about it. I told him that regardless of what this person says or does, don't get angry and don't react. Don't let him or his opinions affect you. Simply love who you are and love him. Know that he is acting out of ignorance of his true self and is not expressing that true self. Just feel love and radiate self-love no matter what.

My student went to the meeting, and sure enough, this person yelled and screamed, beat on the desk, banged on the wall, threatened and intimidated. My student remained calm and loving throughout it all. Eventually, his self-styled opponent gave up. That's because where there is love, there is no opening for anything else to get in.

When a difficult situation arises where someone is angry, you have the choice to get angry too, to argue and fight, or you can love yourself by staying in the vibration of love, not the vibration of anger. Say you've had a wonderful day at work and you come home whistling. When your wife returns home, you ask her in an upbeat way, "So how was your day, honey?" She glares at you with daggers in her eyes and snaps, "What are you asking that for? Can't you just help me get dinner ready?" You could take it personally and raise your voice, shouting back, "Gee, I was only asking you a question! Why do you have to be so grouchy?" And then the argument begins.

The other option is to realize that evidently her day was not as good as yours or she wouldn't be reacting like that. Maybe all day long customers were nasty to her. You cannot change how another person reacts in the moment, but you can change how you respond. That's where love comes in. You can choose to give her a hug and tell her you love her and are happy to help get dinner ready. By being there for her and opening your heart to her, you immediately change the energy in the room. Your love, the love of your real self, is now the sunlight that burns away the clouds for her.

I am not suggesting that you ignore issues that need to be addressed in your relationships. You can and should recognize and acknowledge what needs to be dealt with, but you don't have to be plagued by that same vibration. Don't give power to anyone to take your self-love away. Don't allow their energy to penetrate you and drag you down. When it is raining, bring in the sunshine.

You can take advantage of any troublesome, hostile, or aggressive situation to prove the strength of love. With every breath you take, you can put into practice loving action. To really love in this way requires great awareness, discipline, and self-control. Having intellectual knowledge alone is not enough. You will continue to have problems to solve and obstacles to overcome. The difference now is that you are determined to do all that with love—to become the great gardener in the garden of love that is your life.

Every time you practice loving, you become more adept at loving. Every time you see the result of the power of love, you are encouraged to love again. You will also discover that by acting with love—toward yourself and others—you are able to create more of what you want to see in your life, and create it more effectively, because you are plugging into the very source of your inner power.

FOR YOUR REFLECTION

1. You've learned in these pages that whatever you think about yourself will create your reality. Now take a long look at yourself in the biggest mirror you can find and ask yourself:

- How do I honestly feel about the person I see? What thoughts go through my mind?

- Are those thoughts accurate? Do they reflect the real me?

2. How much do you think you love yourself on a scale of one to ten?

3. The last time someone told you they loved you, how did you feel?

- Were you surprised? Did you feel you didn't deserve their love?

- How do you think your reaction, whatever it was, relates to your feelings about yourself?

4. List the qualities and potential you have for which you are grateful.

- Does this change how you feel about yourself?

- Do you appreciate and value your wonderful qualities and affirm them by saying things like "I'm smart, I'm kind, I'm loving, I'm compassionate"? Or do you hear yourself saying things like "I can't stand myself, I hate how I look, I can never do anything right"?

5. How do you currently express gratitude in your life?

• What evokes in you a feeling of gratitude—special people, nature, music?

• What can you do on a daily basis to express more gratitude, thereby energizing the good that is in your life so you can manifest more of what you want to see?

Chapter Nine

Step Five:
Loyalty

As a warrior on the path to inner power,
I will strive to merge my *body and mind as one* so that
I may discover the *truth* about my strengths and weaknesses
and work to attain *purity* of body, mind, and spirit. I will
learn to *love* myself and maintain *loyalty*
to my goals and purpose . . .

ON THE PATH toward greater inner power, love will inevitably lead you to the next step of loyalty. Loyalty is a supreme act of love. That's because once you truly love yourself, you are committed to taking actions that support who you really are and help you express who you really are. There is no greater way to love your real self than by being it. That is loyalty.

The word *loyal* is derived from the Latin word *legalis*, which means "legal," or pertaining to the law. So when you are loyal to your real self, when you are loyal to true and pure ideas about yourself, you invite the law of manifestation to operate and bring forth your real self. Loyalty is an act of acknowledging this law, an act of recognizing that whatever you are mentally loyal to is bound to take form. Loyalty, therefore, is a lot like gratitude because they are both acts of recognizing or acknowledging an idea. Whatever you're loyal to, you recognize. Whatever you recognize, you think about. Whatever you think about, you manifest.

If you act with your *body and mind as one,* if you know the *truth* about yourself, if you express *purity* and *love,* you have done much to achieve your goal. It is at this point you must exercise *loyalty* to your goal so you can bring your vision to completion—so you do not give up, turn back, regress, or undermine yourself.

Most people's concept of loyalty is that it is directed to something outside of themselves. They think about being loyal to someone else or to a cause. The loyalty I am speaking of here is commitment and dedication to your own life, loyalty to yourself—your real self. Suppose you had a friend who gave you money when you were out of work, gave you a place to live when you had no home, saved your life when you were in trouble, told you to call anytime you needed help. Is that friend worthy of your loyalty? If one day that person asked for *your* support, wouldn't you gladly give it, even if it involved some kind of sacrifice on your part? Most likely, you would do anything you could for this friend. Your loyalty would know no bounds.

If that is what you would do for a friend, what about your real self? What are you willing to do for it? Aren't you deserving of your own loyalty? How much loyalty are you willing to show the infinite part of you that is constantly standing ready, like a friend, to give you everything?

Your Silent Master knows its worth and value, knows it deserves all your love, energy, support, and loyalty. It knows it is truth, purity, and love—*your* truth, purity, and love. Thus, loyalty to your Silent Master is putting your real self forward with confidence, conviction, determination, purpose, power, and love. When you show your loyalty, you are moving as one with your Silent Master.

Before we further explore the concept of loyalty, turn within for a moment and reflect on the quality of loyalty in your life. Have you been loyal toward yourself? Do you dedicate yourself to your goals? Have you been loyal before but are out of practice? Loyalty is like a muscle—the emotional and spiritual muscle that helps get us through each day. And like a muscle, it needs to be exercised in order to stay strong. Let's look now at some of the factors that can contribute to or stand in the way of our self-loyalty.

Be True to Your Own Dreams

When you hear the word *loyalty*, you may think of it as a vague, faraway quality. It's not. Loyalty as a step to inner power involves taking specific actions toward your personal goals, your purpose, your target. So many of us make new year's resolutions—"I want to eat better and lose weight," " I want to exercise," "I want to look for a better job," "I want to meditate every day." How often does our resolve usually last? A few days or maybe a couple of weeks?

Why is it that we give up so easily even though these resolutions represent key stepping-stones to our well-being or to accomplishing our cherished dreams? One reason is that the actions we need to take can feel uncomfortable. It's easier to continue in our old, comfortable way of doing things than to exert the effort to create significant change. Another reason it's easy to give up is that loyalty requires consistent self-discipline—the discipline that allows you to remain committed to two things: yourself and your journey.

You will find that when you start living as one with your Silent Master and commit to worthy goals, all kinds of distractions and new challenges will arise to test your commitment. In fact, the greater your achievement, the greater the tests that come. Only if you love yourself enough to remain totally disciplined and loyal to yourself can you triumph over these obstacles and challenges.

Self-discipline means making good choices so that you don't

stray from your goals when the going gets tough. In order to make good choices, you must be able to clearly identify the things that tempt you away from your plans or have power over you. Athletes in training have to be aware of what interferes with their workouts and avoid those distractions. A person indulging in unhealthy behavior, such as smoking or eating too many sweets, must identify and understand the real reasons they do that before they can correct the condition. Awareness, then, is an important partner to self-discipline and loyalty.

Loyalty to yourself also requires that you recognize when you are tempted to follow someone else's dreams instead of your own so that you can correct course. When you love yourself, you are loyal to what's true *for you,* not what may be true for someone else. As we've discussed, sometimes we make decisions based on what others believe we should be doing, maybe our mother or father or a good friend. Their opinions are not necessarily our truth.

Maybe your parents always believed you should become a doctor. While you had good grades and were certainly capable of getting into medical school, what excited you most was performing music or teaching children. However, because of your parents' expectations you went to school to become a doctor. You ended up living a pretend life, a life that was not a reflection of the real you. After years of living like this, in a moment of honest self-reflection you suddenly admit that you're not happy, that you aren't enjoying your life.

So many people I meet don't end up doing what they really love doing, and then when they reach forty or fifty years old, they wonder why they are unhappy or depressed. That's why it's so important for parents to teach their children from a young age to listen to their own inner voice and make their own choices. You are doing your children a wonderful service when you encourage them to be totally honest and reflect on what is true for them.

Of course, giving your children the benefit of your hard-earned wisdom is a loving action. Yet some parents want to make all their children's choices for them and control their lives. That is not true love; that's imposing their own desires and dreams on their children. Parents sometimes do this because they see their children as extensions of themselves. "I didn't have the opportunity to become a lawyer, so I want them to have that chance," they say. What they may really be thinking at unconscious levels is "I didn't have the opportunity to become a lawyer, so I want them to do that *for me. I want to experience living that life through my children now.*" But your child is a unique being who has a unique life purpose, separate from you. The same principle applies to our spouses and friends. Loving means giving them the freedom to be who they truly are and the freedom to make their own choices.

It is never too late to face the truth that you may be living a life that is not in line with your true self and to courageously make an about-face. Trust that that movement toward loyalty will bring you closer to who you really are. Keith is a good example of this. He was well established in his career as a realtor when he finally admitted to himself that he didn't enjoy it at all. There are a lot of people for whom being a realtor is the perfect fit. But as a young man, Keith went into this business because both his parents were realtors, they were doing quite well at it, and they wanted him to follow in their footsteps. He was never encouraged to examine what his real desires might be.

When Keith learned about the seven steps to inner power, he began to reflect on loyalty to his real self and to his life purpose. By being honest with himself, he realized for the first time in his life that he wasn't happy and felt unfulfilled. When he made the bold decision to leave his career in real estate, new doors opened for him. He had always imagined that he would like to be a speaker and teacher, although the prospect of public speaking scared him.

He ended up getting a job with a high-tech company, where eventually he was presented with that very opportunity. He was offered a job training groups of highly skilled professionals.

Keith knew that his fear of speaking in front of people would hold him back from reaching his full potential. So he made it his goal to practice public speaking so that he could excel at it. That determination paid off. Now he can speak comfortably in front of hundreds of PhDs and is a vice president of a successful Silicon Valley company. By recognizing the truth, being loyal to his truest desires, and then taking steps to confront his fear and overcome it, he set himself free—he broke through to awesome. I'll never forget the look on his face the day he came to tell me about his breakthrough. He had just returned from the first conference where he had to speak. His eyes were sparkling. I could feel his excitement. He emanated joy. That's what happens when you stay true to yourself and your reason for being.

You are here now because you have a purpose. That purpose is part of the entire expression of our universe. To do your part, all you have to do is to be yourself—your true self—and be loyal to yourself with love, support, training, and perseverance. In actuality, doing that is easier than being untrue to yourself. Think how much pain and effort it takes to make yourself live out of sync with your true nature—staying in a relationship that's wrong for you, working at a job you dislike, hanging around with people who aren't uplifting. Being untrue to yourself takes enormous energy. When all of your energy goes to nonconstructive purposes, you feel drained and apathetic. That's why you hear some people use the expression that they are "sick and tired" of what's happening in their lives. Your life doesn't have to be that way.

Keith's story also highlights a key to success that I've touched on before: You can never compare yourself to others, just as you cannot compare a flying eagle to a dolphin or a majestic mountain lion. You are one of a kind, and so you cannot measure your success or your path to success against anyone else's. You are unique, your needs are unique, your contributions are unique.

I have great respect for many people who are described as "successful"—be it Oprah Winfrey or Bill Gates or the president of a country. But I consider that I am as much of a success as they are when I am being true to myself. Their definition of success is not my definition of success. In fact, I do not want their success. I want to have my own success. When I look at this whole planet, I know there's only one of a kind that is me. My one and only purpose is to be a successful me. Your one and only purpose is to be a successful you.

You Are Never Stuck

When you are committed to loving yourself, you know that you are never stuck in one place. You know that at any moment, you can make a new choice to love yourself and be loyal to yourself. One of the main points I've made throughout this book is that your ki energy, the energy that makes up everything in the universe and that you access and use in your everyday activities, is transformative. That is its very nature. It transforms and manifests in different ways, shapes, and forms according to your direction. As you've been learning here, the picture of your body and your environment that you see at this moment is a result of how you have directed your energy up to now. If you change how you direct your energy, you will transform that picture.

You are never stuck, because everything around you is in motion, in constant flux. Since everything that exists as energy can be shaped, you never have to be a victim of what you see, *because what you see is energy that can be changed.* Our oneness with the entire energetic fabric of the universe means we are participating in everything that manifests. We are co-creators of the world we live in.

I've heard so many people say, "I had a goal, I made a plan, but it was too difficult. And everybody told me I was going about it in the wrong way. So I gave up." To that I say: "Why are you giving up? It's *your* dream you are pursuing. It's *your* journey. *You* are the center of your universe. *You* are in charge of composing your surroundings, of directing and producing your own life. So what do *you* really want to achieve?"

I have seen magnificent transformations take place when people break away from the fears and limitations that others try to place upon them. One day at our martial arts academy, the parents of two children came to see me. Their son was athletic and his older sister had autism. The parents were coming in to sign their son up for martial arts lessons and said they thought that their daughter, who was also there, would never be able to take part in that training.

I could see that their daughter, Faith, was also excited by the idea of martial arts and I told them that I felt she could also train. Her parents still didn't think that their autistic daughter could do what was required, but they agreed to let Faith join the class. After several months, the students had to complete a series of tests. One of the tests was that each student had to break a board. Upon hearing this, Faith's mother became very agitated because she was sure that Faith would never be able to do that. I told her mother that the final decision to let Faith continue in the program was up to her and her husband, but I believed their daughter was capable of breaking the board if they allowed me to do my part. I also knew that this process of preparing for and taking the test would be an opportunity for Faith to throw off the limitations others were putting on her and to experience the energizing victory of staying loyal to a goal she had set for herself.

It took some convincing, but her mother finally allowed Faith to take part in the testing event. On the evening of the event, Faith took her place with the other students. When it came time for her testing, to Faith's utter delight her hand broke right through the board. The hall was filled with the uproarious applause of everyone watching—the teachers as well as the other students and their parents. What an incredible and formative experience that was for this young girl. She now knew, from her own direct experience, that she was capable of much more than she or her parents had ever thought possible. She understood that she need not hold herself back because of someone else's fears. She learned to think big—to aim for awesome.

Stay Loyal to Every Part of Yourself

One way to practice being more loyal to yourself is to periodically ask yourself: What can I do to invest in and nurture all the parts of myself—physical, emotional, mental, and spiritual? Go through them one by one and answer that question. How can you stay loyal to the physical part of yourself? You can honor and support your physical body by maintaining a thoughtful, carefully evaluated diet, getting enough sleep, and doing appropriate exercise, for instance. Everyone's body is different and has different preferences and needs for optimum performance, of course. Be willing to consider your body as unique, and pay attention to the effect different foods have on your physical energy.

You can be loyal to the emotional part of yourself by being emotionally honest. If you think about it, whenever you block your emotional energy from coming out, aren't you being dishonest in some way? Aren't you stifling what you are really feeling? I realize there are certain situations where it's not practical to be brutally honest because it will create unnecessary conflict or complicate the situation. I have found, however, that there's usually a way to be honest in spite of potential problems. Honesty doesn't always have to be spoken out loud. Sometimes it's possible to be honest silently. If you can be honest with yourself about what you feel and get support in expressing your feelings in an appropriate way, rather than ignoring or smothering your feelings, you won't be creating emotional blocks that will later show up as emotional or physical difficulties.

How can you be loyal to the mental part of yourself? For one thing, you can exercise your mind. Let yourself be open to new ideas, new learning, new pursuits, new goals. The more you learn, the more capacity for learning you create. Instead of "mindlessly" watching the same TV programs, engage your mind in more stimulating activities that get you off the couch and out of the house.

You can be loyal to the spiritual side of yourself when you take time to connect with your vibrant inner spirit. A willingness to meditate and to commune with your Silent Master allows you to attain what I call the "satellite view." The higher you can get, the wider your perspective and the more you can see. Think of viewing an object or scene from the ground, from the top of the building, from a helicopter, and finally from a satellite. Which of these perspectives gives you the most information about the environment? The view from the satellite. The satellite view is the kind of view you get when you meditate. The information you gather in a meditative state is from the highest and widest perspective, affording you insights into your life and its direction that you can get in no other way.

Clock Your Life Journey

Loyalty also means sticking with your goals and plans in the long term. Our black-belt candidates learn to develop this quality with real-world practicality. Black-belt training is not just about perfecting skills and techniques. The training also involves perfecting emotional, mental, and spiritual skills. As part of their training program, candidates for a black belt in Jung SuWon work toward a five-year goal they set for themselves in their personal lives. They also choose a volunteer service, whether it's working at a hospital, a homeless shelter, or a fire station. They learn to carry the warrior spirit into every aspect of their lives.

When you set a goal for yourself—a program of one year or three years or five years—and then you work toward your goal with discipline and commitment, I guarantee that you'll find a way to make it happen. When I work with my teams on the goals for our businesses and projects, I set a goal of one month or one year or three years, depending on the project, as if that's all the time we have. Why? It motivates each of us working on that goal to summon our inner resources and do everything we can to meet that timeline. It doesn't always work out that we meet that exact timeline, but that's okay. We may adjust our plans along the way, but we start with a firm concept of what we want to accomplish and by when. Setting that goal keeps us in motion and moving toward the finish line.

When athletes prepare to compete in the Olympics, they know the event takes place every four years and therefore they set a schedule for themselves. They dedicate themselves to practicing, training, and striving to reach specific markers along the way within that time frame. They know they have to meet a certain schedule, and they give it their best shot in the time they have to prepare. You can do the same with your own personal and professional goals.

I've also found that acting as if we have only a limited time allotted to us in our individual lives makes us appreciate the people around us, whom we often take for granted. None of us knows how long we have left in this life. When we approach our life in that way, our attitude changes and we become more gentle and compassionate. We treasure the people in our lives and the time we have with them, and we want to make sure they know how much we treasure them.

You don't know when the sun will go down on your life. In fact, when I'm counseling people I will sometimes ask them: "How many times do you think you're going to receive the sun?" By that I mean, how many days do you think you have left to live? I don't ask this to be depressing but as a reality check: "How many days do you think you have left to accomplish what you want to achieve?" So often we procrastinate, and the things that are most important to us get put off and put off because we think we will get to them "someday." When you are loyal to yourself, you realize that you have no guarantee how many more days you have left to receive the sun, and so you have to give priority to your most important goals *now*.

A tool that can help remind you to treasure your time and stay loyal to your goals is to "clock" where you are on your personal life journey. See your life as a twenty-four hour cycle and imagine what time it is right now for you. Let's say you expect to live until you are at least eighty years old (keeping in mind, of course, that you may not live as long as you think you will). If you look at your entire life as being one full day long, that means that when you are forty years old, you are at noontime—halfway through your day. Half of your life has already passed. If you are sixty years old, you are already at 6 p.m. on your life journey.

So each day when you see the clock strike the time that signifies your current age or when you see the sun moving through the sky at that hour, it's a reminder: *That's how much time I have left in my life. Am I spending it developing my inner power and expressing my real self? Am I staying true to my dreams and goals?*

With every breath you take, you become older. And I'm sure you've noticed that as you get older, time seems to fly by more quickly. Have you ever observed how quickly the sun goes down the closer it gets to the horizon? In those last moments, the sun seems to be racing toward its finish line. We run to get our camera and, before we know it, the sun has already set. The same is true in our lives. At some point, your sun will go down quickly too.

So treat each day as an Olympic winner would. What do you have to lose? Know what you really want and give it your absolute best. Create your personal timelines and discipline yourself in working toward them as if you are getting ready for your own Olympics. Each day, the sun rises and the sun sets. Treasure the time you have and use it wisely by staying loyal to your true self and to the life goals that are most meaningful to you.

FOR YOUR REFLECTION

1. Being loyal as a step to inner power means you are committed to being true to your real self and to your own goals.

- List the most important goals you have set for yourself. Next to each one, write down whether you have been completely loyal, somewhat loyal, or not loyal to each goal. Then explain why you chose that answer.

- When you are disloyal to your goals, how do you feel about yourself?

- When you are loyal to your goals, how do you feel about yourself?

2. List ten things you can do to be more loyal to yourself and your specific goals rather than following someone else's advice or measuring yourself against someone else's definition of success.

3. A good way to practice being loyal to yourself is to periodically ask yourself how you can invest in, nurture, and support each of the four aspects of yourself—physical, mental, emotional, and spiritual. Looking at loyalty from that perspective, write down the answers to these questions:

- How can I be more loyal to my physical self?

- How can I be more loyal to the emotional part of myself?

- How can I be more loyal to the mental part of myself?

- How can I be more loyal to the spiritual part of myself?

C h a p t e r   T e n

Step Six:
Sacrifice

As a warrior on the path to inner power,
I will strive to merge my *body and mind as one* so that
I may discover the *truth* about my strengths and weaknesses
and work to attain *purity* of body, mind, and spirit. I will
learn to *love* myself and maintain *loyalty* to my goals
and purpose. I will learn to *sacrifice* in order
to achieve these goals . . .

HOW DO YOU FEEL when you hear the word *sacrifice?* Does the concept seem harsh and uninviting to you, as if you have to give up something you cherish or need? I ask you to consider a different concept of sacrifice, one that will free you to grow in new ways. As the dictionary definition of the word tells us, sacrifice means giving up something for the sake of something else that is better, more important, or more worthy. Thus, sacrifice as a step to inner power is never a loss and always a gain.

Let's start with the fundamental truth that when you are trying to create a lasting change in your life, old habits and new habits cannot exist side by side. You must choose one way of doing things and sacrifice the other. When you set a goal and commit your total loyalty to this cause, you will also need to make decisions about competing priorities in your life. Remember the example I gave of having a goal to train for a marathon race? If you are to be successful in training, attending every party in town cannot be as much of a priority as working out every day.

When your Silent Master gives you a desire, it will never ask you to sacrifice something you need. That is contrary to its nature of love. When you find yourself at a crossroads and you must make a choice of what to hold on to and what to let go of, ask yourself if the so-called sacrifice is really a loss. Usually, the things we give up to achieve a goal are things we no longer need or they are unworthy of keeping. If you give up laziness to keep your workout schedule, is that a loss? If you give up fear to develop public speaking skills, is that a loss? If you give up smoking to become more healthy and set a good example for your children, is that a loss?

In chapter four, you learned about the cycles of increase and decrease represented in the yin-yang symbol and about the truth that every decrease (the black, yin area) carries with it the seed of some new increase (the white dot in the black). Decrease is destined to turn into increase. In keeping with this universal principle, what seems like a sacrifice is never really a loss. It is preparation for a new condition to arise. A recovering alcoholic must sacrifice drinking, but from that sacrifice will come many positive benefits—having better family relationships, being able to hold down a job, and being healthier, to name just a few. Sacrifice helps you get rid of the bad habits and lets you rise to a new level of success and happiness. Sacrifice gives you the tools to succeed.

Interestingly, the word *sacrifice* is derived from the Latin words meaning "holy" and "to make." Sacrifice, therefore, can mean "to make holy." So when you sacrifice your weaknesses, fears, and limitations, you are, in essence, making yourself "holy" by loving your true self and expressing your truth and purity. In expressing more of your true self, you will never lose anything you need. You will only gain what makes you more pure and more free.

This is a joyful, expanding process, no matter how painful the sacrifice may appear on the surface. When you are facing a sacrifice, don't think of it as something you are being forced to give up. Instead, focus on why you want to give it up. You're sacrificing so that you can grow and develop, so that you can be the best person you can be. You're investing in yourself and your happiness.

Making Choices That Match Your Goals

There are times in life when circumstances drastically change and we are forced to make a choice that involves a sacrifice. Maybe we have to change our lifestyle to recover from an illness or we have to move because our spouse was offered a new job in another city. But responding to change isn't the only kind of situation where sacrifice comes into play. Sacrifice can also be proactive. You can willingly give up certain attachments and states of mind to make room for newer, healthier options.

When we talk about sacrifice and letting go, we can view it on two levels—physical and mental. Letting go involves both outer activities and inner attitudes. First, let's consider what it means on the physical level of action. Are you familiar with the story of the monkey who put his hand through a hole to grab on to a piece of food on the other side? Suddenly, he sees something nearby that he wants even more. Tightly grasping the food, he tries to pull his hand out of the hole so he can reach for his new goal, but he can't get his hand as well as what he's holding through the hole at the same time. He keeps pulling and tugging, trying to get his hand out. The monkey doesn't realize that he won't succeed until he lets go of what he is grasping. He has to surrender the old object before he can claim the new prize he has his eye on.

How does that lesson apply in your own life? You may say, "Of course, I'm willing to change. I want to turn over a new leaf. I want to become who I really am." You may feel highly motivated. Yet your willingness to change must also be accompanied by a strong motivation to sacrifice, to let go of, what doesn't support your new lifestyle. As in the story of the monkey, the old and the new cannot exist side by side.

You may want to lose weight or lower your cholesterol levels, and maybe you've started to do so. But what happens when the rubber meets the road? How do you respond when you realize that your old eating habits, like meeting co-workers every Thursday after work for all-you-can-eat pizza and beer, have to go permanently in order to win your goal? If you're trying to stop drinking alcohol, won't you have to let go of your old habit of meeting your friends in bars? If you need to get up early to prepare for an important job interview, can you afford to be a couch potato and stay up late watching TV? In other words, you may have to consciously and intelligently choose to end an activity you are now engaged in so that you can pursue your true goals. You'll have to make a decision based on what's most important to you now. And you'll have to select your environment carefully to help keep your commitment pure and strong.

Be prepared that as you change, you may not be able to keep the same relationships. In fact, you may not want to keep them. You have to choose what you will be loyal to and what you will sacrifice. It comes down to the fact that *you* are the one who has to take charge. If you want to quit smoking or drinking heavily and a friend at work says, "Come on, let's take a break and have a smoke" or "Let's get together for a drink," you're the only one who can say, "I'm sorry but I've made a decision not to do that any longer." You may risk losing that friend because you're not partying to her standards, but you will have to decide right then and there: "Is this friend worthy of me and what I want for my life? I'm trying to get my act together and she can't see how important that is to me."

When you are working with sacrifice as a step to inner power, also be aware of the subtle influences others may have on you. Have you ever noticed that your behavior changes when you are around certain acquaintances? Perhaps with some people you tend to be honest, outgoing, and expressive, and with others you tend to be insecure, insincere, and a bit phony. Do you find that you can't be yourself when you are around certain people? If so, ask yourself if you really want to keep relationships that encourage you to express traits you are trying to eliminate from your life and that do not reflect the real you.

In short, always use your power of choice to protect your freedom to be your true self. When you decide to eliminate some element of your environment, you're powerfully affirming: *I have the power of choice. That is not who I am, and therefore I choose another environment, one that does support who I am.* When you do this, you are taking charge of your life in a big way.

Letting Go of Dangerous Attitudes

Now let's look at another dimension of sacrifice—letting go of attitudes that block our progress. Letting go of attitudes is just as essential as letting go of unhealthy activities or saying goodbye to people who hinder our progress. In fact, unless you let go of certain attitudes, your physical letting go won't last very long. This concept is related to the inner power step of purity. When you let go of an attitude that is sabotaging who you want to be, you are also purifying your world of a habit pattern that has kept you hostage to limited thinking and limited living.

It's a common misconception that most of our attachments center on objects or people. The truth is that our attitudes and feelings *about* objects are more binding than the objects themselves. For example, we may become attached to an object, person, or situation (even if we complain about it) because we like feeling comfortable, we fear change, and we don't have the courage to take initiative on our own. Maybe we stay with a domineering boyfriend, girlfriend, or employer, even though doing so is keeping us stuck in a rut. In cases like these, fear is the real attachment, not the person.

If suddenly those people are removed from our lives but we still have not let go of our fundamental fears and have not developed the strength to stand up for ourselves, we'll just become attached to the next domineering boyfriend or girlfriend or employer that comes along—and continue to complain about them. That's because the thoughts we keep in our mind rule over us as long as we allow them to stay there, and they continue to produce the same results.

Here's a different example that shows how attachment to a self-defeating attitude can harm us. Let's take the attitude of resentment. Resentment is a common mental attachment most of us have to deal with at some time or other. If you think about the last time you were resentful, you probably thought you had every right to feel that way, and it didn't occur to you that this attitude was hurting you—or you would have already stopped being resentful.

Let's say someone at work received a promotion you thought you deserved. Maybe you became resentful and said to yourself, "It isn't fair that she got that job. She isn't as skilled as I am. I should have that job, not her." You may even have thought, "I hope she fails, because she doesn't deserve this." Then you allowed those thoughts to roll around in your mind with lots of strong feeling attached. The fact is, the feeling of resentment is totally unnecessary, and by feeling it, you only make yourself a prisoner of that feeling.

That person got the promotion because she helped create it or attract it with her own thoughts and emotions. At that moment, she manifested the job instead of you. However, because she got that particular position does not mean you won't get one commensurate with your worth. By resenting her, you are buying in to two dangerous beliefs. First, you're denying that you have the power to create your own improved situation. And second, when you stay resentful, you are essentially affirming that you missed out on the one and only opportunity you will ever have to get a promotion. If you believed there were still possibilities open to you for advancement, you would stay open and expectant, not resentful.

So what if that person got promoted to the position you wanted? That's no reason to limit yourself. You can still use your creative power to get what's right for you. Maybe it's not the right time yet for your promotion. What if the reason you didn't get that promotion is because it would keep you from being available for a better job? If so, hanging on to resentment can actually shut down your options.

Here's an example of how a scenario like that can play out. Say Jack and Steve are both applying for a promotion. Their manager gives Steve the promotion, and Jack is very disappointed. Jack knows he's more capable than Steve and he can't understand why he didn't get the job. He thinks it's unfair. What Jack doesn't know is that his manager is already planning to give him an even better position than Steve has, but she can't let him know about it yet.

Unfortunately, instead of letting go of his resentment and keeping a positive attitude or even going to talk to his manager about it, Jack lets his bitterness get the best of him. He becomes irritable and starts to make snide comments, putting down Steve and his other co-workers.

This goes on for a couple of weeks and Jack's boss starts to get complaints from others in the office. "I've never seen this side of Jack before," she thinks to herself. "Maybe I was wrong about him." So when the better management position she had in mind for Jack opens up, what does she do? She decides to interview other people for it.

Jack's resentment has sabotaged him. His bitterness and lack of trust in how his own inner power can shape his life robs him of the golden opportunity that was waiting for him. It's as simple as this: harboring negativity and an ugly attitude will chase people and opportunities away, and cultivating positivity and an optimistic attitude will attract great people and opportunities to you.

In effect, when you resent, you are hanging on to underlying negative beliefs, which keep you in a state of loss. As long as you cling to resentment, you are not free to use your thoughts and emotions to create your own good. Those false beliefs will create more negative situations, encouraging you to feel more resentment, and the cycle will go on and on until you stop it. How do you stop it? By understanding why you must let go of those mental attitudes and then using your will and intelligence to do so—keeping in mind all the tools you've learned in this book so far, including the all-important five principles of mental conduct we covered in chapter three.

A Tool for Staying on Track

Resentment is only one example of an attachment that can hold you back unless you let it go. You can think of other negative attitudes, such as anger, self-pity, criticism, or whatever you might be holding on to right now, and look at the underlying beliefs at the root of those feelings, just as I did for resentment. By honestly examining the beliefs that underlie those limiting emotions, you will more clearly see how letting them go can create dramatic changes in your life.

Sacrificing the negatives that draw us off our path is not a one-time choice, of course. It takes a continual recommitment to our goals, especially when the going gets rough. For example, people who want to lose weight can get frustrated after a while when they don't see the results they expect, and they may end up falling back into their old habits. One tool that can help you stay on track is to audit yourself every week. Knowing that you'll face challenges and need to make adjustments on the path toward your goals, instead of criticizing yourself and giving up out of frustration, put in place a process of self-assessment. Start by simply asking yourself every week: How did I honor my commitments this week?

If you don't audit yourself when you are trying to create change in your life, before you know it your negative habits can gain momentum again and take over. Don't let that happen. Be honest. Be loyal to yourself and remind yourself of why your goals are important to you and why you're committed to sacrificing for them.

The practice of self-assessment will take you a long way toward making progress in your personal as well as professional life. When I am choosing who among the employees in my companies to promote, I carefully watch their attitudes and responses in different kinds of situations. When the situation at work is good, anyone can perform well; but I want to know how people perform under stress and when times are tough. I encourage those I work with to learn from challenging situations by self-assessing.

When you use a process of self-evaluation while working toward any goal in your life, whether it's losing weight or getting a promotion, you make time to ask yourself at regular intervals: How did I do in that tough situation this week? Am I falling back into negative habits and attitudes that I committed to let go of? Am I keeping the promises I made to myself, my manager, my team, or my family? Am I being arrogant, thinking I can easily handle small digressions from my original goal? Do I need to get support?

Building in time for this kind of self-reflection allows you to take a step back and objectively look at yourself and the situations in your life from a 360-degree perspective. Only when you do that can you make necessary adjustments as you work toward creating a new vision of yourself.

Creating a Future Unhindered by the Past

Once you dedicate yourself to achieving goals that go beyond your present concept of yourself, you may also find that you have to work hard at letting go of your past. You have to sacrifice the old story to make room for the new vision of yourself. Doing that may require forgiveness on your part because forgiveness is the way we release the past. *You cannot change a situation if you keep holding on to it with negative emotion.*

Even though we've all heard that forgiveness is a key to growth, it can be hard to sacrifice a feeling of injustice and let go of past hurts and wounds. Start by reminding yourself that forgiveness does not mean you absolve anyone from wrongdoing. The wrong that was done is still wrong and will always be wrong. Rather, forgiveness helps you release the pattern so it will not repeat itself in your life. You don't want to be terrorized by the memory and the burden of a past incident, do you? Then let it go.

When we keep thinking about and regretting something that happened in the past, we continually re-create it in our minds. We literally charge those memories and patterns with the energy they need to stay alive. We saw this in the story I shared of the woman who had been raped three times. She had to learn to stop revolving in her mind pictures of herself as a victim in order to stop magnetizing people into her life who wanted to complete that picture and victimize her.

I understand the dynamic of letting go of past hurts very well.

It was an important part of my early training under my martial arts master. My childhood circumstances—being resented by my mother, beaten by my father, shunned by my entire village, and laughed at for aspiring to be a martial artist—would have overwhelmed me with self-pity had my teacher not taught me to take charge of my own life and refuse to be a victim.

It was wrong of my father to get drunk and beat me again and again. It was wrong for my family to treat me as bad and unworthy merely because I was a female. It was wrong for them to criticize me unjustly, shame me, and try to crush my natural desires and goals. But what if I had made the decision to hate my family for the rest of my life instead of forgiving them and focusing on my training and goals? Hate has the effect of solidifying what we hate, making it more real and enduring.

Hate will energize and strengthen any situation, just as love will, but it will energize and strengthen it negatively. So hating my family would have made their abuse more enduring and more vibrant. It would have made the abuse more likely to manifest physically and emotionally in my life, not only from them but from others I would attract. My release from that oppressive environment was only made possible by *not hating*.

Have you ever met someone who felt mistreated or who experienced a traumatic event when they were young, and now at thirty or forty years of age or even older they still look back and blame the people involved in that circumstance? That event may have happened when they were fifteen, and now it's more than fifteen years later, but they still tell the same old story to themselves—and to anyone who will listen. Many years have passed, but they still act like a victim, waving their flag of surrender.

Sometimes people who come from a situation of child abuse, and who continue to hate their abusers without doing anything to dissolve the pattern of hatred they carry, later find themselves married to an abuser. What's interesting about this is that even after the abused person ends the marriage, he or she will often end up in another abusive relationship. We can clearly see the power of energetic patterns at work here. Since the energetic pattern isn't being removed from the person's consciousness, merely leaving the marriage does not end the problem, and so it automatically repeats. Forgiveness is the key here because it gives us the freedom to create the new unhindered by past impressions.

Letting Go of Guilt

As we take the next steps toward accessing greater levels of inner power, even more challenging than forgiving others may be forgiving ourselves for the part we feel we played in past events. Yes, people do make mistakes and hurt others. We all make mistakes. But you never need to condemn yourself or anyone else over and over again for those mistakes. Learn whatever you need to, let it go, and then move on to create a new reality.

The main obstacle to forgiving yourself is guilt. If you think back to your childhood, didn't authority figures usually deal with mistakes or misbehavior by condemning the behavior and the person engaged in it? We weren't taught that a mistake is an opportunity for education or an opportunity to see what doesn't work so we can create a better solution.

One of the most important steps to take in letting go of the past and getting ready for a new life is to realize that you don't need to feel guilty forever and ever. Guilt has a purpose for a little while. It makes you feel remorse and shows you that you need to change. Once you take action to create change and make amends, guilt no longer serves a purpose. In fact, at that point it's obstructive because it keeps you trapped in the energetic pattern you want to get beyond.

If you are holding yourself back by feelings of guilt that you find hard to let go, realize that your guilt is a feeling about something that's over. Whatever the issue or mistake, identify the lesson you learned and vow not to repeat that behavior. Affirm that the circumstance is not a part of the true you now. It happened, it's over, it's gone. Now let it go.

FOR YOUR REFLECTION

1. When we commit to specific goals and changes we want to make, we also have to prioritize how we will use our time and identify what we may need to sacrifice, to give up doing.

- Review the goals you said you were not completely loyal to in the loyalty exercise in the last chapter. What are you doing that is preventing you from reaching those goals?

- Is there a state of mind or attitude you are harboring that is preventing you from reaching your goal? What is it?

- How can you let go of those activities or attitudes?

2. You can weigh the advantages and disadvantages of sacrificing or not sacrificing an action or attitude by filling in a table like the one below. The example below shows how someone might weigh the advantages and disadvantages of sacrificing or not sacrificing when deciding whether to continue eating ice cream while going out with friends.

	Advantage	Disadvantage
Sacrificing	I will reach my goal of losing weight much more easily.	I might feel embarrassed eating a fruit bowl instead of eating ice cream like everyone else.
Not Sacrificing	I get to eat whatever I want.	If my eating habits stay the same, I won't lose weight.

- Create a chart like the one above for a sacrifice you are considering.

- Based on what you wrote down, is the sacrifice you have in mind worth it? Why or why not?

3. Forgiveness is key to creating your future free of energy patterns from the past. When we don't forgive or when we harbor resentment, we perpetuate past energy patterns as well as the condemnation or guilt that accompanies them. We cannot change the past, but we can acknowledge that it is over, learn from it, and move on.

- Is there a situation you still think about where someone hurt you and you have still not forgiven that person?

- Is there something you have done to hurt yourself or another person that you have not forgiven yourself for?

- For each instance, write down (a) exactly what you learned from that situation and (b) what behavior or choices you have decided not to repeat again.

Step Seven: Patience

> As a warrior on the path to inner power,
> I will strive to merge my *body and mind as one* so that
> I may discover the *truth* about my strengths and weaknesses
> and work to attain *purity* of body, mind, and spirit.
> I will learn to *love* myself and maintain *loyalty* to my goals
> and purpose. I will learn to *sacrifice* in order to achieve
> these goals and seek *patience* in my ways so that I
> may ultimately become the master of my life.

IF YOU'VE TAKEN to heart what you've been reading so far about the seven steps to inner power and engaged in some serious self-reflection, you've most likely already made headway toward your most cherished goals. Let's say you have chosen a meaningful goal and committed to making sure your body and mind (your actions and thoughts) are aligned and acting together as one as you work toward that goal. You've been honest with yourself so you could learn the truth about your strengths and weaknesses. You've worked on purifying, or eliminating, from your life the weaknesses that have stood in your way.

You've also been careful to love yourself by finding ways to give yourself support—physically, emotionally, mentally, and spiritually. You've determined to remain loyal to your purpose and have begun to sacrifice, or let go of, the unhealthy habits and attachments that have sabotaged even your best intentions. You are well on your way to achieving your goal.

What do you still need so you can reach your destination and complete the transformation you desire? Patience is the final step in the creative process. It is here that impatient people may backslide and lose the benefits of all their hard work.

One of nature's most beautiful symbols of patience is the transformation, the metamorphosis, of the caterpillar into a butterfly as the caterpillar's "beingness" changes drastically from one form to another. Perhaps there is a situation in your life that needs this kind of radical transformation. If you desire to make a change as great as that, the quality of patience is essential.

For a distinct period of time, which cannot be rushed, the caterpillar ingests food so it can grow to a certain point. When that point is reached, the caterpillar then forms a cocoon, where it must wait for another period of time. A transformation occurs in the quiet cocoon that also cannot be rushed or disturbed. Then at last, at the appointed time, a butterfly emerges, a different creature altogether from the caterpillar, who then reproduces so that the cycle can begin all over again.

As the caterpillar goes through this transformation, isn't there patience and trust going on? The laws of nature that enforce the caterpillar's miraculous transformation are absolute. All that's required in cooperating with the law is patience and trust. The laws of manifestation that govern our being are just as absolute. We must likewise have the patience and trust to let them work.

My martial arts master in Korea taught me a wonderful lesson about patience when one day he gave me the assignment to "watch that cocoon." I took one look at the gray-brown lump in front of me and said to myself, "What is that? It looks like it's dead. Why does he want me to watch it?" I didn't understand why he would have me do such a thing. It seemed like a waste of time. My master assured me that much was happening that I could not see. "Learn to be patient," he said. "Watch."

So that's what I did. Finally, I thought I saw the tiniest of movements. Putting my ear up to the cocoon, I was startled and thrilled to hear small scratching sounds. Something really was alive in there! After so much waiting, I was finally going to see it emerge. But it, whatever "it" was, seemed to be taking forever. Although I waited for many hours, it still didn't seem able to break out of its cocoon. After a few days passed, I decided that it must be having trouble and I had better help it. Very carefully I peeled away the outer layer of the cocoon to set free what was inside.

Out stepped a butterfly. It walked around and fluttered its wings. But that's all it did. It could not fly. My master knew at once what I had done without me even telling him. I had interfered with the butterfly's process of transformation. The effort required to break out of the cocoon is a necessary part of the butterfly's development. In my ignorance, I had interfered with the work it needed to do to prepare for a life of flying. My master wanted me to learn patience, of course. He also wanted me to understand that everything in life requires right timing. It takes patience not to interrupt the natural flow and unfolding of events. That applies to any situation, whether we are working toward a particular goal or whether we want to jump in and help a friend. We always have to take into account whether the timing is right.

Keep the Power Turned On

True patience means you keep the power turned on as you knowingly wait for what you've been working toward to appear at its appointed time. Patience is knowing the truth and expecting the truth to manifest. This knowing and expecting is part of the process of being your Silent Master. Thus, when you express true patience, you think as your Silent Master thinks.

Say you've been trying to get pregnant for a long time and are ecstatic that it has finally happened. You have a little morning sickness and at last you get over that. After three months, do you say, "Where is my baby? I'm ready to get this over with. Let's go." At five months, at six months, at eight months and beyond, you have to be patient until the baby's development is complete.

Let's take a totally different situation. Say your home was destroyed in a flood and has to be rebuilt. After the builders have started working on it for a couple of weeks, is it realistic to ask the builder, "Where is my home? Where's the finished living room? Where's the kitchen? When can I move in?" You don't do that because you know how much time it takes to build a new home. You've done your planning, you've sacrificed to make it happen and stayed loyal to your goal, and now you are patiently awaiting the conclusion of the project. When you are manufacturing a new product, you know you have to move through stages one, two, and three before you can move on to stages four, five, and six. In order to avoid a lot of frustration and anxiety about the project and instill patience, you carefully chart where you are in the process.

Your life is also a work in progress. It takes time for you to grow and mature. Everything requires a certain time frame for its completion. Although we may not be aware of the timing of the processes in our life, those stages still exist and we are moving through them. This may be a much more far-reaching view of patience than you are used to. You may think of patience as what you need when you have to wait for an hour at the doctor's office or when you have to wait in a long line at the grocery store. What I'm talking about is a whole different level of patience. Sometimes you have to be patient for years to achieve certain life goals. When you are in the middle of that process, you can't allow yourself to get easily disappointed with every delay and use that as an excuse to give up.

Unfortunately, patience in today's world is not something that comes naturally. It is a quality we usually need to acquire. In part that's because we are bombarded by the media with images and slogans of instant gratification. "If you want this, call this number or go to this website right now." Modern technology, too, has encouraged us to expect instant gratification. When we want food, we can have it instantly at the supermarket or at a fast food drive-through. There was a time, though, when we had to patiently watch over our crops as they grew, milk the cows, pump the water, harvest the crops, bake the bread, and so on. There was no room for impatience in that life.

You can take advantage of all of today's marvelous resources, technology, and advanced communication tools to help you along the path toward your goal. There is no substitute, however, for old-fashioned patience in your pursuits. Not everything will simply be handed to you or spoon-fed to you. More often, you will have to go through a process to reach your goals, a series of many steps that seemingly start and stop.

Remind yourself that the plateaus you reach on the way are not ending points. They are just plateaus. It's important to know that you can still be in motion while you are seemingly at rest. When things don't seem to be in motion, be sure to keep your mind moving.

Patience is not passivity. Remember, when a seed is underground and invisible to our eye, it is nevertheless moving aggressively. And though you don't see the motion of the plant growing when it is above the soil, that is nevertheless what is occurring. In the same way, not all of your progress will involve radical physical activity. Sometimes your faith and desire will be all you see in motion. But that is motion, you are going somewhere, and you will need patience to ride the process through to the end. The total picture will always be a little outside your scope of vision and you will have to trust in the power of your real self to guide you to and through the unseen steps involved.

Make Use of Every Stop and Step

When there is a delay in reaching your goal, remind yourself that it's not over 'til it's over. As long as you're here, the opportunity to reach your goal is here. We sometimes don't realize that an unexpected turn of events, which can at first seem frustrating, may nevertheless be part of the overall plan that is leading us to our goal—as long as we stay loyal to ourselves and learn at each stage. Every event in your life is teaching you something. To take the straightest path to your goal, make use of every little stop and step along the way.

As an example, look at the biblical story of Joseph (the young man with the coat of many colors), who went through many tests and trials before becoming the most powerful man in Egypt besides Pharaoh. When he was a boy, Joseph's brothers became jealous of him, and during a journey they abandoned him and left him to die. He eventually landed in prison and became a slave. Do you think Joseph knew that these events would eventually lead him to a position of political power in Egypt? It's more likely that he was tempted at first to be angry and resentful. After all, everything had been taken from him—his family, his wealth, even his freedom.

Yet all along the way, through all that happened to him, he retained his integrity, valued his inner worth, and remained loyal to himself. No matter where he landed, he expressed positive qualities instead of indulging in impatience or resentment, and for his unique talents he was elevated to a position of power, serving as the right-hand assistant to Pharaoh. So the unfortunate events he experienced were nevertheless leading somewhere better. Fortunately, he did not indulge in impatient resentment but held on to his integrity until a much better end was in sight.

When I was cleaning toilets at my first job at the hotel and people were calling me all sorts of unsavory names and saying things like "Go home, you chink," I had to learn to use that as motivation. Whenever they did that, I said to myself, "Thank you for motivating me, for energizing me, for fueling me to try harder, to do better, to focus more. Because I know someday I am going to be a martial arts master and teacher and I am going to make a difference in people's lives." I knew that if I was to succeed, I could never let those people have power over me. I continually affirmed: "They are not my God. I know who I am and what I am. I know the direction I am headed in."

Achieving my goals didn't come instantly. Step by step, I had to create for myself the conditions that would allow me to give birth to my dreams. I had to practice patience as I used all the tools you're learning here—tools like awareness, balance, visualization, self-honesty, the determination to love, forgiveness, loyalty. I said earlier that when people ask me, "When did you feel you had your first success in your life?" I answer without hesitation, "When I was cleaning toilets on my first job." I knew that that job was only one step on my journey and not the final destination. I knew I wouldn't be doing that forever. It was an opportunity to learn and get experience. More importantly, it was an opportunity to train my mind.

When I was cleaning those bathrooms and I would see the dirt and dust, the rotten food, the stains, the grime and the gunk, I would say to myself, "That's like the constant criticism I received all those years from the people in my life who told me I couldn't pursue martial arts because five thousand years of tradition said I should be learning how to cook and sew instead. That dirt is like the sneers and the condemnation I get now from people who call me names and treat me like trash. I will not let them have power over me. I'm going to work on erasing that right now." As I scrubbed, I saw those problems being cleaned out and washed away. I never lost sight of what I wanted to achieve, and I saw my scrubbing and cleaning as clearing the way for what I knew in my heart would one day become a reality.

So whatever condition you find yourself in right now, concentrate on developing positive thoughts and feelings rather than focusing on your current circumstances. You will not be stuck in those circumstances forever. Know who you are and who you want to become. Focus on patience and take charge of your life. Instead of complaining, use each stepping-stone along your path as an occasion to develop your inner qualities, to polish the diamond that is you. Practice success by keeping your vision of your goal in your mind and heart and by developing the mental traits that will get you where you want to be.

The Importance of Making Your Own Breakthroughs

Patience, then, as a step to inner power means we know and expect that bringing any worthwhile goal to fruition is a process and therefore we are patient in seeing the work through. That's a key lesson for children to learn from a young age. Parents can be tempted, however, to do everything for their children. They love their children, which is wonderful, but loving also means allowing children to put forth the effort to learn their own lessons and accomplish their own goals.

By dominating and controlling children, we can rob them of the opportunity to discover their own abilities, strength, and beauty. If we do not let them fall down and get back up and continue to work through the process of accomplishing something *on their own*, they won't develop the quality of patience they will need in much greater measure in later life.

Have you ever observed parents at sporting events who are trying to coach their children from the sidelines? This happens in martial arts classes too. Some parents can't sit still. As they impatiently watch their young children train, they are constantly shouting to them, "Remember to stand straight!" or "No, not that way! Look at how Billy is doing it." This would be comical except that their comments are usually discouraging not encouraging. The children end up looking over at their parents and feeling terrible because they don't think they are measuring up. The parents are actually interrupting their children's natural growth process and interfering with what their children need to do in order to become adept at their art. So when this comes up, I go over to the parents and politely ask them, "Do you have some shopping or errands you would like to do and then come back when we are through with our lessons?"

It's important for children to understand that no one else can train for them. They have to put in the effort and determination themselves and reap the rewards for themselves. I tell them: "No one can eat for you or sleep for you, right? Well, no one can learn for you, no one can fail for you, and no one can win for you either. *You* must go through the stages of training and the stages of your life yourself. That is the beauty of patience and all the steps to inner power. You have to go through your own life experiences so that you will gain the understanding, wisdom, and strength that are meant for you."

Achieving an important goal in your life will not happen overnight, and it's not meant to. You try and you fail, and you try again. In the process, all sorts of thoughts may spin through your mind. "Oh my God, this is embarrassing. It looks so simple. Why can't I do it? Maybe I'm not cut out for this." You become wrapped up emotionally in the doubt or fear or self-criticism.

When this happens in our martial arts classes, I say to my students: "That's okay. Relax. Don't focus on why you weren't able to do that just now. Instead, you should feel great that you are even trying this. Some people are afraid of trying anything new at all. So be patient. The fact that you have courage and are already starting to learn these skills is beautiful and powerful. That means you are on your way. Please feel proud of yourself!"

Thomas Edison, America's prolific inventor and innovator, is famously quoted as saying, "I have not failed. I've just found 10,000 ways that won't work." He didn't say, "Oh, I've messed up so many, many times! I'm such a failure. I might as well give up right now. This is hopeless." Instead, he understood that he was in the middle of a process and that he was constantly learning and improving as he moved closer to his goals. As long as you are engaged in the process, even if you feel you are falling backwards, you are actually moving forward. As long as you are taking action, you are making progress.

Remember, we live in a universe that's made of vibrating energy. Energy is in motion. We're part of that energy, and we need to express motion in our creativity. Some people never take their goals beyond "information collecting." They talk about what they want, they think about it, they look into it, they dream about it, they read books about it, they admire it. But they don't do anything about it. Fulfilling your goals requires an energy process to manifest. It requires motion and activity.

As you have seen, the obstacles you will meet as you move toward your goals always have a purpose. Like the butterfly, by patiently fighting and breaking through obstacles, you are building your strength. As you work with each of the seven steps to inner power, you are gaining the skills you need to accomplish your life's work. You are becoming a true warrior. You may not realize that you are gaining important skills and strength, but that is exactly what is happening as you do challenging things in life, whether they are physically, emotionally, mentally, or spiritually challenging.

Persistently Follow Your Inner Instincts

Another lesson we can draw from the caterpillar's transformation is that to reach his goal—a process seeming fraught with obstacles, risks, and delays—he must remain persistent and consistent. He does not give up as he follows his inner instincts, as day by day he goes about his routine crawling from leaf to leaf.

In addition, since he is completely in tune with his own life force, he knows when it is time to stop that activity. When his change is complete, he does not attempt to cling to the old form simply because it is familiar. He lets go of the old, again trusting and following his instincts (just as you can choose to follow the instincts your Silent Master gives you). He willingly endures a plateau of seeming inaction while a wondrous, creative transformation slowly manifests.

Is the caterpillar patient? Yes, but you could also say he's being true to himself. Isn't patience simply being true to yourself? Isn't transformation simply being true to yourself? Isn't letting go simply being true to yourself? When you are true to yourself, you let in the energy that transforms you and everything around you, fulfilling the goal you set, planned, and followed through on.

Look again at our caterpillar. Imagine trying to explain this miraculous transformation to someone who had never heard of it. You talk about a wormlike crawling bug who eats plants but knows when he's eaten enough and when it's time to stop, who knows how to wrap himself with threads that he makes from his own body, who then disappears inside this sealed encasement, who then secretes chemicals from his own body, which let him disassemble and re-form again—not as a drab crawling bug, but as a multicolored winged creature that flies through the air. That doesn't sound like it should be possible, does it? Such creativity, such intelligence, such imagination.

How about the tiny little brown nut that holds within it the awesome power to transform into a majestic tree, or the unborn bird who pecks away at his shell hundreds of times for no other reason than to be born—for no other reason than to be who he is. He patiently follows the life force as far as his purpose directs. Think about the cells from a man and woman that unite and know how to express themselves as eyes, hands, hair, legs, feet, ears, and a brain that processes intangible qualities like feelings, thoughts, desires, and love. Or the giant stars exploding into elements that know how to form as the metals and minerals of planets. If all this does not begin to convince you how creative the universal life force is, think again.

That very power and creativity is your own. Those miracles we take for granted every day are pictures of your own life force in motion. How can you ever insist that you are nothing, nobody, with no purpose, no talent, no opportunity when you possess energy like this? This magnificent power is your inner power to access and put into action in your life with patience and persistence.

Be Compassionate with Yourself

The patience we are required to practice as we work toward our goals is not just patience with the process and events that unfold but also patience with ourselves. Don't forget to give yourself a pat on the back. Congratulate yourself and celebrate when you see that you have made even a small amount of progress.

Most of us can easily recognize when other people are being mean to us instead of loving and respectful or when they are tearing us down instead of being supportive. But, as I touched on earlier, we don't always recognize when we are treating ourselves that way. Do you address yourself lovingly or is your inner dialogue constantly self-critical? Do you know when you are being abusive to yourself? Part of practicing patience is being respectful toward yourself and forgiving yourself. If you catch yourself being impatient, doubting yourself, or constantly criticizing yourself with self-destructive energy, you know it's time to have a heart-to-heart talk with yourself. Go to a mirror, look yourself right in the eyes, and remind yourself that you deserve to attain the goals you have set for yourself.

You have spent many years forging the personality you have and you are now looking truthfully at what aspects of yourself have to go so you can express your true inner power. That takes time and requires plenty of compassion along with patience. There's an old saying, "don't go away mad, just go away." As you work on replacing old self-concepts with more unlimited ways of thinking about yourself, the same thing applies. You don't want to spend your energy criticizing and arguing with yourself. Instead, you can act from a clear, calm center within yourself to quietly take charge of directing your life.

Think about the compassion you feel for a little wounded bird separated from his mother and the shelter of his nest. Give yourself the same compassion as you go about healing yourself. You, too, have been separated from the shelter of your true self. And you, too, deserve the same patient love and care that will return you to safety.

You Are the Co-creator of Every Moment

The seven principles of inner power are all intimately related to each other. You cannot fully practice one without including the others. To practice body and mind as one, you need to practice truth, purity, love, loyalty, sacrifice, and patience also. In reality, there is no such thing as "today I'm working on purity." Each and every day, you work on all these principles.

As you make these qualities real in your everyday life, know that what you are really practicing is your beingness, your self-hood, your Silent Master. You're not asking yourself to be anything that's not real or not possible. Your Silent Master is your only true self. As you are joyfully and expectantly practicing these seven principles, you are becoming your Silent Master.

Unlike the caterpillar, we do not usually make our transformation in the darkness of a private space. Ultimately, each of us is alone. Each of us is a private individual. But we are alone together in a world of many people. Thus, our transformation is worked out in the world classroom. Much of our learning will be out in the open, composed of many small actions that will, step by step and moment by moment, create changes just as startling as the caterpillar's transformation. One painting is composed of thousands and thousands of brush strokes. In addition, because we are not alone in this world, our actions are guaranteed to affect others. What we learn about ourselves often comes from our interaction with others. Our relationships are our teachers. We learn from each other.

There's a story I'm fond of that illustrates how we, as individuals, can make our own hell or heaven when we attempt to live together. This is hell: Ten people are seated at a dining table. They have abundant food in front of them, but the chopsticks they are required to use are all three feet long. When they try to eat, they discover that the size of the chopsticks makes it impossible for them to feed themselves. They are all starving, quarreling, and fighting. They think only about themselves, want to take from each other, and feel frustrated and miserable.

This is heaven: Ten people are seated at the same dining table with the same chopsticks. They are all happy and well fed and are having a wonderful, peaceful time together. These people are unconcerned that they cannot feed themselves with the long chopsticks because they are using them to feed each other. The needs of every individual are met because they cooperate with each other and work together.

Everyone and everything that comes into your awareness was drawn there by you. Therefore, as you go about your daily life, you can do so with grace. Rather than regarding yourself as a victim, serenely see yourself as the creator and co-creator of every moment. As individuals we create our private worlds, and collectively with other members of the planetary body we create our larger world. Regard every situation, then, private or global, as an opportunity to practice the truth of your being in your thoughts and actions. Concentrate on yourself. When you are being the best person you can be, don't be surprised if you find others transforming along with you.

FOR YOUR REFLECTION

1. List five goals in your life that you have already accomplished. For each goal, write down how long it took to achieve that goal.

2. Has impatience ever caused you to give up on a goal or interfered with you achieving that goal?

- What happened?

- How did you feel?

3. Describe or sketch the most important goal in your life right now.

- How long are you willing to wait for this goal to be realized? One year? Two years? Five years? Ten years? Longer?

- Is that goal worth any amount of time you might have to wait?

4. Our relationships are the classroom where we learn and apply key life lessons. Thinking about your relationships, write down situations you frequently encounter where each of the seven steps to inner power can help you in your interactions with others. Here are some examples.

Body and Mind as One
Example: "When my mind and body are one, I can listen to my spouse instead of letting my mind wander and making him feel that I'm not hearing what he has to say."

Truth
Example: "When I am honest about and express my true feelings, my children will know that I care about them and that I

am committed to treating them as individuals" or "When I am able to see and admit my mistakes, I won't be so defensive and get into so many arguments with people at work."

Purity
Example: "When I stop being jealous of my colleagues who seem so successful, focus on improving my own abilities, and have more confidence in myself, there will be less tension in the office and the people around me will notice how much more productive I am."

Love
Example: "When I love myself more and embrace myself with love and compassion, I will not scare away potential partners by being so needy."

Loyalty
Example: "When I am loyal to my goals and faithfully devote myself to working on them each week, I will feel fulfilled and won't take out my frustrations on my family."

Sacrifice
Example: "When I stop smoking after a twenty-year habit, I will present a better example of a healthy lifestyle to my children."

Patience
Example: "When I am patient with the team members I supervise at work, they will be happier, better trained, and more productive."

PART THREE

Movement *and* Meditation

Chapter Twelve

Energize Your Life

How DO YOU FEEL right now? Do you feel strong, energetic, and ready to take on whatever challenges come your way? Do you keep your body as well as your mind in good shape? Do you engage in activities that test your limits and enable you to experience your natural energy flowing through you? If not, I encourage you to consider some kind of physical activity, in whatever form is right for you, as another key to unlocking your inner power and reaching your life goals.

Up to this point, you've learned primarily about the mental and spiritual concepts in the martial art I teach as you've explored the practical principles for successful living drawn from the practice of Jung SuWon. But remember that Jung SuWon is the art of uniting body, mind, and spirit in total harmony, and therefore we emphasize all three of those areas—physical development, mental discipline, and tapping into the wisdom and power of your original self.

For my martial arts students, physical training is a practical and tangible way to put the important mental and spiritual principles into practice. Mind and body are one. Therefore, when practicing the physical form of Jung SuWon along with the seven steps to inner power, we are doing so to develop our whole being. The physical training creates a mindset and skill set that brings about success in all areas of life. So the physical training is really life training. We use the physical form as a training ground to grow, develop, and master all areas of our lives.

I would like to introduce you now to some of the fundamentals underlying the physical aspect of Jung SuWon so you can see why unlocking greater levels of your own physical power—in a way that is appropriate for you—will propel you toward achieving your goals fearlessly and creatively. While the examples here are largely taken from martial arts, you will see how these principles apply to any form of physical training you choose and to your own path of self-mastery and life success.

Why Not You?

Let's start with my motto and the cornerstone of inspiration for my students as they progress through their stages of training: "He can do, she can do, why not me?" That saying has several meanings that apply equally to mental, spiritual, and physical power. First, on a physical level it means that physical strength and the knowledge of self-defense derived from physical training are available to both men and women. No one is limited by gender.

Strength is one of the ideas expressed by your Silent Master. Whether you are a man or a woman, strength is part of your original self. Since strength is an idea, can the idea of strength be "stronger" in a man than in a woman? No. Ideas don't come in degrees of intensity. Because I know that strength is an idea belonging to my original self, I know that I am not limited by my four-foot eleven-inch, ninety-pound body when defending against an attacker of much greater size and weight. I've proven that over and over again, and so have my students.

Second, "He can do, she can do, why not me?" means that the principles of Jung SuWon are practical. The increased physical strength and self-defense skills that come from Jung SuWon martial arts training are certainly practical rewards. They reduce fear and weakness and build true confidence and self-esteem. Tae Kwon Do, Shotokan Karate, and Kung Fu are all similar in the origins of their basic forms. However, the quality of physical mastery in Jung SuWon depends directly on the extent to which students apply the mental and spiritual training.

Learning the martial art moves and forms, learning how to spar effectively with an opponent, and demonstrating extraordinary physical feats, such as breaking bricks with their bare hand, require that students consistently put into practice the same practical keys you've discovered in this book—the seven steps to inner power as well as the principles of awareness, balance, visualization, commitment, and all the principles of mental conduct and right thinking. Students who are training in Jung SuWon focus all those ideas within the parameters of this structured art form, and they measure their progress in a disciplined manner.

The training, then, is a feedback system, letting them know where they stand in taking control of their mind and body and where they can improve. When people train in a martial art, they become keenly aware of their weaknesses and their negative thoughts and emotions because they are making greater demands on their body and asking themselves to perform and interact with others in ways they may have considered impossible before.

Earlier in this book, I gave the following example of how body, mind, and spirit work together, and we can now bring it full circle. I said that in martial arts training, the ability to powerfully kick and punch is worthless unless students direct their physical activities with mental focus and confidence. Having great physical strength will not help in the least if your mind is full of paralyzing fear and you lack self-esteem. You must conquer fear and weakness within yourself before you can conquer a foe outside yourself. On the mat as well as in life, you must free yourself from limiting, self-defeating states of mind.

Students in training are eventually required to break a thick board, and later even one or more cinder blocks, with their hand or foot. That is not a feat of physical strength, though it may seem so. It can only happen if they direct their inner power, their ki energy, through their hands and toward their target with absolute focus, determination, and inner fire. As part of their training, students also focus on their personal life goals and on overcoming the inner obstacles to achieving them. In fact, when students go through their qualifying tests to break a board, I ask them to write on their board a specific, detailed goal they have set for themselves. "You are not merely breaking the board," I tell them as they concentrate on the task at hand. "You are breaking through the obstacles to your goal."

Those obstacles may be fear or doubt or lack of confidence, perhaps even overconfidence or arrogance. Students become very aware of what their limitations are because these weaknesses have surfaced during their training, and they have been working to overcome them. (Please note that breaking a board is *never* something you should try on your own and should only be done in a proper setting with proper training and instruction. I am using this example as a metaphor for the determination and striving each of us must summon to "break through" the mental blocks and outer obstacles that try to prevent us from reaching our goals.)

A third meaning of "He can do, she can do, why not me?" is that when you set a goal, you know that you must do the work *for yourself*—"he can do, she can do, why not *you*?" Yes, those victories you've seen others attain—you can attain them, too, by doing the work that is required. Why not you? You have awesome resources of power at your disposal.

Too many people shortchange themselves. They discount their

own abilities as they hang on to fear, self-doubt, or self-condemnation. Don't be one of them. In reality, the only thing that separates you from your victory is the effort it takes to get there. You *can* succeed—unless you are too mentally or physically lazy. You can do whatever you want to do if you are willing to take the necessary mental and physical steps and persist and persist until you win. Once again, you have to differentiate between true, honorable goals and mere fantasies and daydreams. Know the difference and go after your valid goals with every ounce of energy you have.

The Skill of Gentle Persistence

The physical challenges Jung SuWon training presents are designed to draw out our not-so-desirable character traits so we can see them face to face. Our intense and challenging life experiences often do the same—they reveal to us the weaknesses we need to overcome. Facing those limitations isn't comfortable or easy. That is why I refer to the person seeking their real self as a warrior. You are not a warrior only when you learn to physically fight. You, as a seeker, are also a warrior because the "not-self" traits you may have identified as "you" are not necessarily easy to relinquish.

It takes time and persistence to challenge a weakness in yourself and shed unwanted characteristics. That process may feel like a struggle, like warfare. Keep in mind, though, as I said in the chapter on purity, that your weaknesses are only shadows of your real characteristics. The war against a shadow does not have to be waged with force. It's not sensible to aggressively fight against something that's insubstantial, is it? Instead, the war can be won by gently and consistently embodying the real idea about yourself that you want to express more of.

"Gently" does not mean "weakly." Gentleness is its own kind of force. Do you know the fable about the contest between the sun and the wind? They each tested their power by attempting to make a man walking along a road take off his cloak. As the wind ripped and tore at the man with tremendous force, the man only drew the cloak tighter and tighter around him until the wind finally gave up and challenged the sun. The sun, however, showed no "force" at all. Gently and persistently, it burned brighter and hotter. Finally, in the heat of the day, the man released his hold on the cloak and took it off. When you are trying to change yourself and shed old habits that may be clinging to you like an outworn cloak, you will get further by being like the sun—by gently and persistently being who you are in truth.

During your "warfare" to overcome limitations and reclaim your inner power, remember, too, what we discussed in the section on truth—remain unimpressed with the evidence of your material senses. Keep in mind that the material picture you see outside of yourself is never the source of truth. It is simply a picture of what you've been *believing* to be true—a picture you can choose to change when you change your thinking. Whatever shadows you see are not the real you. You are not limited.

Sharpening Your Ability to Observe Reality

Another powerful skill we cultivate in martial arts training is observation. It's not by accident that many martial art forms incorporate the qualities of animals such as the tiger, eagle, crane, bear, turtle, or monkey. To extend their fighting skills, the original martial arts masters observed and imitated traits they admired in those animals—survival, self-defense, courage, discipline, patience, and others traits.

We do not live in natural surroundings the way people did thousands of years ago, so you may not be able to directly observe the basic truths and primal ideals embodied by nature's creatures. You, the modern warrior, may have to imitate others who have learned the way before you. However, you will still need to observe as much as the original warriors did. The skill of observation is a powerful, essential weapon in self-defense as well as in everyday life.

How do you observe? By being here, now, so that you are undistracted by thoughts of the future or the past, which don't exist anyway. Now is all there is. For instance, in martial arts as in life, knowing that an opponent is getting ready to strike a blow or sensing that you yourself must strike a strategic blow to defend yourself is only possible by being in the now moment.

Do you ever wonder how martial artists who are sparring can quickly and efficiently respond to the movements of their opponents? To a large degree, it is because they practice being observant in the present moment. To effectively respond to an opponent, we can't be distracted or caught off guard. The same is true in a challenging situation at work or at home. When you are dealing with an emotional or mental assault, you need to be mentally and spiritually in the right place at the right time to respond with the right word or action suited to that particular situation. The only time that can happen is *now.*

Let's say you have an important business negotiation you have been working on and you are ready to close an incredible deal, but the customer is shrewd and intends to manipulate you. You will only be able to detect his strategy by being undistracted and in the present moment. If your mind is unfocused, you will walk into the mental trap he has set. The ability to sense what is happening around you is the best offense and defense you can have. It is the reward for disciplining yourself to live in the now, the only reality.

The Extra Oomph to Push Through

Now that you understand a few of the principles underlying the physical aspect of Jung SuWon, let's return to the questions I asked you at the beginning of the chapter. Do you feel strong, energetic, and ready to take on whatever challenges come your way? Do you keep your body as well as your mind in good shape? Do you engage in activities that test your limits and enable you to experience your natural energy flowing through you?

Even if you do not consider yourself someone who is "physical," I encourage you to demand more challenging physical activity from yourself in some form. Deep inside, you know you need it. Your body and mind are one, and one without the other will not be able to do its job. You can think of your body as a dish holding precious liquid (representing your energy, mental capacity, and spirit). If the dish is broken, it cannot hold the liquid, which will leak out and disappear. Simply put, if you don't keep your body in prime condition, your body will limit your ability to achieve your dreams and goals.

Not everyone's physical capabilities are the same, and you don't have to train in martial arts. Find a type of physical training that works for you and meets your needs and schedule—one that builds up and maintains your strength and one that challenges you to ongoing levels of physical mastery. Jogging may be right for one person while yoga or dance is a better choice for another person.

If you have a medical condition that makes it challenging for you to attempt rigorous training, you can still engage in some form of physical conditioning, under the supervision of your doctor, to keep your body in the best shape possible. Within the scope of your physical abilities, there is always something you can do to challenge yourself. A student of mine is paralyzed from the waist down. He has been in a wheelchair since he was eleven years old. Yet, because of his determination and indomitable spirit, he has consistently trained in the aspects of martial arts he is capable of doing, and he is now one of my master students. Be sure, of course, to use your common sense too. If you have a cold or the flu, you must get better before doing intense physical activity. If you have a broken leg, you must let it heal before you can use it again.

Beyond the health benefits of staying physically active—and the fact that keeping your body in good shape also gives you a clear mind—engaging in some kind of physical training while you are working toward your life goals gives you that extra oomph to push through and beyond any obstacle. That is because challenging yourself to develop greater physical capabilities sends a message to your mind that you want to stretch and go beyond what you previously thought was possible. As you discipline your body to push beyond previous thresholds and gain more power and ability to perform, your mind responds in kind by opening up and expanding more of its power and ability to perform. That is energizing and empowering.

In other words, since body and mind are one, the strength and power you gain through your physical discipline carries over to your other activities. If you are not physically active, you will tend to get tired and feel lazy. You'll feel as if you don't have much energy to pour into your goals. On the other hand, when you are physically working out, through whatever form of exercise you choose, you'll feel more mentally clear and energetic—and you'll have exponentially more creativity and power to apply to your life goals. You will always achieve optimal results in every aspect of your life when your body, mind, and spirit are all strong, sharply focused, and powerfully engaged.

FOR YOUR REFLECTION

1. You can apply the simple but profound truth "He can do, she can do, why not me?" to any situation or goal in your life. How would you apply this phrase to yourself as you work toward your next goals in these areas of your life:

• Your career?

• Your relationships?

• Your health and fitness?

• Your spiritual development?

2. When you push yourself to greater levels of physical ability in whatever form is right for you, your increased physical energy and discipline will also carry over to other parts of your life and propel you toward your goals.

• What physical activities are you engaged in on a regular basis now?

• What can you do to challenge yourself to gain greater levels of physical power?

• What kind of physical goals will you set for yourself?

Chapter Thirteen

Making Your Life
a Meditation

How do you define meditation? Some people say that in order to meditate correctly you must cross your legs in a certain way. Others say you have to breathe in a certain way or meditate for a specific period of time or focus on a certain object or idea, or on nothing at all.

I have found that having strict rules about what to do and what not to do makes it hard for many of us to even consider meditating. Not everyone, for instance, can meditate with their legs crossed. If some people try to meditate that way, they will spend the entire meditation thinking to themselves, "Oh my gosh, my leg is killing me!" That's counterproductive because the pain is bringing negative thoughts into their mind, making them feel uncomfortable and creating anxiety rather than peace.

In addition, in our busy twenty-first century all of us are concerned about managing our time and our schedules. How many of us can find the time to sit quietly somewhere for an hour each day? If you think you have to meditate for an extended period of time every single day, you may give up before you even give it a try. Each of us is unique, and so we have to adapt our personal meditation style to our individual lives, to our lifestyle and our surroundings.

Moving Meditation

I would like to introduce you now to a different way of understanding what it means to meditate and how you can incorporate this important and beautiful practice into your life more effectively. First and foremost, meditation, as I describe it, is meant to bring you tranquility and peace of mind, to clear your thoughts so you can hear the thoughts of your real self. To me, when you are totally engaged in the present moment and are at one with your real self, without extraneous thoughts entering in and disturbing you, you are meditating. You can achieve that state of oneness while in quiet meditation, but you can also achieve it when you are in the midst of any activity. That means you can be meditating anytime and anywhere.

If you are a ballet dancer and are completely engaged in your performance, one with the flow of the music and the sublime movement of the other dancers on stage, you are meditating. If you are in the audience watching the ballet and are so captivated by it that you feel one with the cadence and rhythm of the performance, you, too, are meditating. You're not thinking, "I've got to get home and pay my bills" or "I need to be sure and pick up those clothes from the dry cleaner tomorrow." By this definition, you can be meditating while you are immersed in watching a spectacular sunset, listening to a flock of birds fly gracefully overhead, taking in the beauty of a garden in full bloom, playing the piano, laughing with a child, cooking a special meal for a friend you haven't seen in a long time, or even playing a sport.

In fact, I refer to the physical practice of Jung SuWon as a "moving meditation" because the training requires you to focus your mind on specific ideas and qualities as you move. No movement in martial arts should be without direction or without thought. All movement is focused and purposeful. It involves concentration. The Latin roots of the word *concentrate* come from *com*, meaning "together," and *centrum*, meaning "center." To concentrate, then, means to "draw everything to a center."

The truth is that any activity that you do with your body and mind as one in the present moment can be a moving meditation as you draw your thoughts and actions to a central focus. "If that's true," you may ask, "what about when I'm balancing my checkbook or cleaning house or building a bookshelf?" Yes, those things can be moving meditations, too, if you carry them out in the spirit of "body and mind as one."

A good way to help you make your daily activities a moving meditation is to write down or say aloud (or silently to yourself) an affirmation that reflects how you will engage your mind and body as one as you carry out a specific activity. Here are a few examples so you get the idea.

While you are driving, you might say: "I am keeping a calm, attentive state of mind as I patiently and persistently move toward my destination."

At work: "I am focusing on this particular project this morning and will not allow anything to distract me."

Engaging in sports: "I am totally focused on the present moment and am aware of all my surroundings—the field, the other players, the ball."

Cooking a meal: "I am expressing my love for the people who will receive this meal, including myself."

Eating a meal: "I am focusing on loving myself as I nourish my body."

Sharing affection with your significant other: "I am focusing completely on this moment together, on the beauty of who you are and the joy you bring to my life."

Playing with your children: "I am giving all my attention to you at this moment and am expressing my gratitude to you because you remind me of how much joy there is in life."

Singing or dancing: "I am one with the music as I send this loving message from my heart to the world."

Reading a book: "I am learning all I can and becoming a better person in the process."

Conducting an interview on TV: "I am peaceful and fulfilled and I am ready to share my ki energy secrets with the world."

So you can see that any activity that brings you into deeper communion with your real self in the present moment, whatever gives you a sense of peaceful unity, is a moving meditation. In essence, the goal in Jung SuWon is to *make our whole life a moving meditation.* With the right frame of mind, the right view, and the right attitude, you can move as one with your Silent Master at all times, thereby creating harmony, beauty, peace, right action, and love right where you are, right now.

Energizing Your Goals with Meditation

Many of us have come to think of meditation as taking time out from the busyness of the day to sit quietly and calm our thoughts.

There are many reasons to meditate in this way. You may simply want to relax and feel the pleasure of your mind expanding. You may want to visualize a desired outcome. You may want to acquire information outside your current conscious awareness. Meditation is certainly a way to clear, cleanse, open, and expand your thinking, and I'll talk more about a suggested technique for that in a moment. First, let's explore how to apply the art of meditation to mindfully focus on our goals.

It's easy to get caught up in the hustle and bustle of the day and forget to focus on the goals that are actually most important to you. To keep those goals foremost in your thoughts and feelings, they need to become a part of your very heart and soul. Having gone through the exercises in this book, by now you have some kind of list of your short-term and long-term goals. In order for those goals to take form, you need to feed them—to energize them. One way to do that is to review your goals every morning before you start your day.

When you wake up, instead of feeling the pressure to jump out of bed and get going, plan a little extra time to consciously connect with your real self and your inner power before rushing into your day. If you have a backyard, you can go outside and feel yourself among the plants and trees and birds, feel the breeze, and experience the light of the rising sun. Or you can imagine those tranquil scenarios in whatever space you do have. Then spend a few minutes in quiet meditation feeling the peace of your original self, your Silent Master.

You can calm yourself using the suggested technique on the following pages or some other practice that works well for you. Once you are calm and at peace, go over your list of goals. You can recall your goals mentally or write them out again on a piece of paper. Perhaps your goal is to express more affection to your spouse, to show more patience with a difficult co-worker, to exercise for an hour today, to stay on your diet, to find a good real estate agent who can help you find a new home, or to spend more time with your children. During this quiet meditation time, visualize yourself successfully completing the next step toward your goals in as much detail as you can.

To give a simple example, say your goal is to pass the course you are currently taking with flying colors as a step toward qualifying for a better job. As part of that course, you may have a project coming due. During your daily meditation, *see* yourself energetically and passionately completing that project and enjoying the process. *Feel* what it's like to have finally finished it so you can move on to the next phase of your plan. If your goal is to improve your relationship with your children, during your meditation hold that intention in your heart. In your mind's eye see yourself interacting with your children with patience, understanding, and compassion. Feel the smile that lights up their faces when you do so.

If the only time you have for yourself in the morning is your daily shower time, remember the shower meditation from chapter seven (pages 173 to 175), where you can turn your daily shower into an effective meditation with the intent to cleanse and purify yourself of negative thoughts and feelings and then set your intention for the day. When you keep your goals and values in mind during meditation, you are, in effect, fueling them and ensuring that they won't slip away from you.

Once your goals are clear and focused in your mind, the next step, of course, is to spend your day in charge of your goals. Instead of going about your day waiting to see what will happen, make time to act on your goals. When you take charge of your day, you take charge of your life. You won't wait for something unusual to happen in order to express patience and kindness toward a family member, for example. If your goal is to pursue a new career, instead of waiting for a job to open up in the company you want to work for, you will proactively rewrite your resume, learn any new skills you will need, practice for an interview, and contact the HR department of the company with a well-written and creative letter. If you are passionate about starting this new career, you won't even entertain the notion of procrastinating. You will put your passion into action every day.

Meditating with Your Silent Master

One of the most profound kinds of meditation is intentionally calming your mind to listen to the thoughts of your real self. Whether this type of quiet meditation is done formally or informally, it always consists of two steps. The first step is to affirm to yourself that you and your Silent Master are one and to fully expect that the necessary information you seek (or the serenity, clarity, cleansing, etc.) will come to you. Remember, your Silent Master consciousness operates over and above both your conscious mind and subconscious mind. Therefore, whatever your purpose in meditating, your Silent Master can effectively penetrate your conscious or subconscious mind to guide you appropriately. The second step in meditation is to quiet your mind, to put aside all clamoring thoughts and feelings. In that stillness, you can know and hear the guidance you seek.

Sometimes after meditating, you will find that you immediately get a sense of knowing. Sometimes you will have to repeat your meditation many times to bring about the result you desire. When your answer doesn't come right away, be patient. Often, the answer will arrive at just the right time.

During busy days, all you may have time for before plunging into the next challenge is to simply close your eyes and take a few deep breaths as you connect with your own inner power. That's fine. You may also like to adopt more formal meditation procedures to strive for deeper states of consciousness, such as the meditation

I outline below. This kind of formal meditation can be one of the most satisfying, rewarding aspects of your life.

Our ordinary thinking process is so noisy that we rarely get a chance to experience other aspects of our consciousness unless we make a focused effort. There is much to say about the subject of meditation, and I go into greater detail in my other books. For now, I'll describe a simple meditation that can relax your mind and help you experience more expanded states of awareness. (Please do not do this meditation while you are driving or if you are in a situation where you need to pay attention to external matters.) Before you meditate formally, list some questions you want to pose to your Silent Master. You can pose one of those questions in step 7.

The following steps are suggestions. If any of these suggestions are not comfortable or not possible, please feel free to adapt these steps in whatever way works for you. If it is hard for you to sit on the floor while meditating, for instance, try sitting in a chair, lying down, or even walking. Whatever method you choose, always keep the two objectives in mind—first, to know your unity with your Silent Master and expect that the necessary information (or other desired result) you seek will come to you and, second, to quiet your mind.

1. Sit comfortably and calmly on the floor, on a flat pillow, or, if that is not comfortable, sit on a chair with your feet flat on the floor. If you use a pillow, try to keep one especially for the purpose of meditating, one you do not use for anything else. I recommend silk or cotton ones.

2. If you are seated on a pillow or the floor, one classic meditation posture is to bend your right leg and place your foot under your left thigh. Bend your left leg and lift the left foot onto your right thigh. (If this hurts, don't force it. Do this

only if you are able to comfortably.) Your legs should now be crossed with the right on the bottom and left on top. Next, bend your body forward, arch your back, and then straighten up.

3. Place your right hand, palm facing up, gently on your lap. Place your left hand, palm facing up, on top of your right hand and bring your thumbs together. Your thumbs should be barely touching, as if you were holding a sheet of paper between them.

4. Straighten your neck. Your head should be level, not turned up or down, and your earlobes in line with your shoulders. Close your mouth and place your tongue on the roof of your mouth.

5. Sitting quietly, close your eyes and focus on your breathing. Your breathing should be gentle and quiet. Someone sitting next to you should not be able to hear you breathe. Breathe in deeply through your nose, hold your breath as long as you can comfortably, and then exhale slowly and softly. Repeat this until your breathing is slow and gentle.

6. Let any worries, concerns, or clamoring thoughts and feelings flow away. Initially your conscious mind will feel uncomfortable when you ask it to suspend its habitual thinking processes (or, more often, worrying processes). It wants to keep thinking and will try to do so. Just watch these thoughts. Don't hold on to them, follow them, or fight them. Let them simply come and go. If necessary, tell them you'll pay attention to them later, but not now (usually the thoughts go away when they have this reassurance).

Right now, you want to strive for the most pristine purity and clarity of consciousness you can. To do that, you must suspend your customary thinking processes. Eventually, you will feel your mind getting clearer as your thoughts slow down and simply settle like dirt in a pond. This clarity will increase as you practice this exercise on a regular basis and get acquainted with who you are apart from your stream of thoughts.

7. Now, in this stillness, you can choose to visualize the successful accomplishment of your goals (as I described previously) or pose a question or problem to your Silent Master. Ask for guidance. Ask in whatever way feels right. Your Silent Master is listening.

8. Then relax your mind and let all new thoughts flow freely to you. They will have a different feeling altogether from the clamoring ones you may have experienced in the beginning. These thoughts are messengers of one sort or another, responses swimming into your awareness as a result of your meditation. Do not become attached to any of them. Let them come and go as they will. Pay attention to them, but do not force yourself to analyze or think about them. You can analyze later with your conscious mind.

The Joy of Listening

Earlier in this book, I asked you to pose this question to yourself: "Who am I?" I encourage you to pose that same question to your Silent Master in formal meditation. It is one of the simplest yet most profound meditations you can undertake. Who is more qualified to tell you who you are than your real self?

When you reach step 7 in the meditation above, ask, "Who am I?" lovingly and sincerely, with your whole being. You can repeat the question several times, slowly and with full concentration. Then listen. Listen until you know that you've listened long enough for now, even if you feel you haven't received an answer. You have. The answer will begin to manifest in many different ways as long as you continue to repeat the meditation.

When you ask, "Who am I?" you are subtly asking two questions: "Who am I, the self that I know?" and "Who is the 'I' of the Silent Master?" Of course, you and your Silent Master are one, and this meditation helps bring about that realization in the truest sense of what the word *realization* means—to "make real."

"Who am I?" You are asking something incredibly simple really—something profoundly natural, something as close as your own being yet as infinite as the universe. Your Silent Master knows this question and knows the answer. Now you, through your meditation, can also begin to know and to "make real" your unity with your real self.

That meditation requires much repetition and patient listening. The understanding that results from it doesn't usually happen all at once. The expanding sense of knowing your real self can be so subtle that you don't realize you're getting it until you have it. Meditating with your Silent Master in this way can also be full of joyful surprises. The meditation will enlighten you in its own way, in its own time. Imagine the joy of day by day growing into a fuller understanding of who you are—who you really are and the power you really have.

It's that simple. Your real self awaits your knowing. Let it come slowly, like the dawn, if it must. For now, you, the warrior on the path of uniting body, mind, and spirit, can know *I am one with the universal life force. I am creative energy. I have the power to fulfill my dreams. I can break through to awesome.*

1. Any activity that you do with your body and mind as one in the present moment, without extraneous thoughts disturbing you, can be a moving meditation.

• Pick three activities that are part of your weekly routine and write down a statement you can say aloud or to yourself to affirm your intention of carrying out each activity with a sense of peaceful unity—with body and mind moving together as one. For example:

   At work: "I am focusing on this particular project this morning and will not allow anything to distract me."

   Cooking a meal: "I am expressing my love for the people who will receive this meal, including myself."

2. Consider experimenting with a form of quiet meditation, such as the short morning ritual described on pages 259 to 260 or a more formal meditation like the one outlined starting on page 262.

• Before meditating, think about a problem or issue you are dealing with and write down a question you want to ask your Silent Master when your mind is sufficiently stilled.

• Always keep in mind these two steps as you begin meditating:

   (1) Affirm your unity with your Silent Master and fully expect that the necessary information (or serenity, clarity, cleansing, etc.) that you seek will come to you.

   (2) Quiet your mind, putting aside clamoring thoughts and feelings, so you can hear the thoughts of your real self.

E p i l o g u e

The Infinite Possibilities
of Your Inner Power

MY PURPOSE IN SHARING the teachings that have been handed down to me is to help you expand your vision of yourself and awaken to the enormous potential you have within you to shape your life. My only desire in life is to help you become all you are meant to be by sharing what has worked for me. Even if what I have shared changes the life of one person, I will be thankful.

As you learned early in this book, your life is exactly the way it is now because of the way you have answered the question "Who am I?" That's because how you answer that question determines what choices you make every moment of every day. By now I hope I have convinced you to think of yourself as you truly are—a creative, powerful being who can break through the limitations that you may have imposed upon yourself or allowed others to impose upon you.

The power that created galaxies, that formed oceans of space, air, water, and consciousness is the very same power that flows through you, beats your heart, and gives you consciousness. As it flows through you every moment, you literally become a co-creator with this limitless energy. That is your birthright. *Claim it.*

It doesn't matter what has happened to you before or what choices you have made in the past. You can decide right now to take control and change the picture of your life. You can choose to be who you want to be. You can experience the joy and fulfillment of creating your life anew each day as you go after your goals with the focus, determination, and enthusiasm of an Olympic athlete.

You now have in your hands the practical tools you need to accomplish your breakthrough, including the six core truths that will help you identify with your original self and stay focused on your real capabilities, the five principles of mental conduct that will boost your confidence and free you from self-defeating ways of thinking, the essential tools of balance, awareness, visualization, and meditation, and the all-important seven steps to inner power. As you have seen, these steps are a way of living and being that empower you to express, in every aspect of your life, the qualities of your creative and powerful self and to become a positive force in the lives of those around you.

All you need to do now is put these tools into action consistently and with determination. Don't give up! All the tools and techniques in this book were born out of my own personal experience. So I know that they will work for you as you work with them, and I look forward to hearing your personal stories of overcoming.

Remember that the most important event in your life is happening right now. The most important choice you have is the choice of what you will do with the present moment. You don't know if you will have a tomorrow, if you will have another year or another thirty years. The only time you can guarantee is now—the present moment.

I believe in your beauty, I respect your unique purpose in this world, and I support with all my heart your growing awareness of who you truly are and what you are capable of achieving. You *can* break through to awesome. You have infinite possibilities before you. You have tremendous power. What will you do with it?

Acknowledgments

Every day, every sunrise, I thank God for guiding me toward my life's purpose and for every living breath I take. Every day is a new gift.

I thank my martial arts master for teaching me from the time I was a young child, for believing in me when nobody else did, for showing me how to develop my inner strength, and, most of all, for teaching me to never give up.

I thank all those I have come in contact with for the opportunity to learn from them. I thank those who have brought challenges my way. You were my greatest teachers, for through those challenges I have become stronger and I have gained freedom.

I thank Scott Salton, Paul Newman, Angela Sommers, Thomas Saunders, Peter Maguire, Agape Kim, Michael Fell, Hope Winter, Holly Chamberlain, and all my loyal students for taking to heart and applying my teachings and for constantly striving to learn and to improve their lives and the lives of those around them.

I am also grateful to my talented editorial, publishing, marketing, and sales teams for believing in my work and supporting me in so many ways.

Finally, I thank every one of my wonderful readers. You continually inspire me. My love is with you always.

Dr. Tae Yun Kim is a martial arts great grandmaster, author, and motivational speaker. She began her training at the age of seven, defying five thousand years of tradition prohibiting girls from learning the martial arts in South Korea. Against all odds, she became the first female martial artist in South Korea and one of the highest-ranking martial artists in the world.

As head coach, she led the first-ever U.S. women's Tae Kwon Do team to a gold medal at the Pre-World Games in Seoul, helping pave the way for women to compete in martial arts in the Olympics. Dr. Kim went on to found her own school of martial arts, aimed at overcoming limitations in every area of life, and she teaches at her academy in the San Francisco Bay area. She is also the founder and CEO of a leading high-tech Silicon Valley company and has won numerous distinguished awards for her achievements and humanitarian service.

To learn more about Dr. Tae Yun Kim and her work, visit:

taeyunkim.com
facebook.com/DrTaeYunKim.CEO
youtube.com/DrTaeYunKim
twitter.com/tykcando